广东财经大学学术文库

退耕还林政策与黄土高原地区农户可持续生计：

基于生产率和效率的实证研究

GRAIN FOR GREEN PROGRAM AND SUSTAINABLE AGRICULTURE AND RURAL LIVELIHOODS OF THE LOESS PLATEAU IN CHINA:

Empirical Studies with Measurement of Productivity and Efficiency

李　莉◎著

经济管理出版社
ECONOMY & MANAGEMENT PUBLISHING HOUSE

图书在版编目（CIP）数据

退耕还林政策与黄土高原地区农户可持续生计：基于生产率和效率的实证研究 = Grain for Green Program and Sustainable Agriculture and Rural Livelihoods of the Loess Plateau in China：Empirical Studies with Measurement of Productivity and Efficiency：英文/李莉著 . —北京：经济管理出版社，2021.5

ISBN 978 - 7 - 5096 - 8003 - 2

Ⅰ.①退…　Ⅱ.①李…　Ⅲ.①退耕还林—林业政策—研究—中国—英文 ②黄土高原—农户经济—可持续性发展—研究—中国—英文　Ⅳ.①F326.20 ②F325.15

中国版本图书馆 CIP 数据核字（2021）第 100765 号

组稿编辑：郭丽娟
责任编辑：郭丽娟　张广花
责任印制：黄章平
责任校对：王淑卿

出版发行：经济管理出版社
　　　　　（北京市海淀区北蜂窝 8 号中雅大厦 A 座 11 层　100038）
网　　址：www. E - mp. com. cn
电　　话：（010）51915602
印　　刷：唐山玺诚印务有限公司
经　　销：新华书店
开　　本：720mm×1000mm/16
印　　张：9
字　　数：139 千字
版　　次：2021 年 7 月第 1 版　　2021 年 7 月第 1 次印刷
书　　号：ISBN 978 - 7 - 5096 - 8003 - 2
定　　价：78.00 元

Preface

The Loess Plateau, with the most serious soil erosion worldwide, is among the most poverty – stricken areas in China. Land reclamation, overgrazing and deforestation for growing foods and subsistence needs aggravate both the economic and environmental circumstances for the farmers, and brought about significant negative externalities, in the past decades. The Chinese government responded with a program called Grain for Green program (GfG, also known as the Sloping Land Conversion Program) in 1999. The program is intended to help peasants escape the poverty trap through financial support, technical assistance, and institutional improvement so that agricultural production improves and surplus labor shifts to off – farm jobs, with sloping marginal land being set aside. By addressing environmental conservation, food self – sufficiency and wellbeing enhancement simultaneously, the ultimate goal of the program is to help promote sustainable agriculture and rural development in the target areas.

Indicators of productivity and efficiency measure the ability of decision – making units to generate more outputs with less inputs, given existing technology and/or environmental conditions. In the context of a land retirement program like GfG, it is essential to improve the productivity and efficiency at both the farm and farm – household level in order to achieve sustainable

◇ 退耕还林政策与黄土高原地区农户可持续生计：基于生产率和效率的实证研究
Grain for Green Program and Sustainable Agriculture and Rural Livelihoods of the Loess
Plateau in China: Empirical Studies with Measurement of Productivity and Efficiency

agriculture and rural livelihoods in the future. While previous studies have focused on the impact of the program on either farm or off – farm production, we are pondering the need to consider the farm and off – farm activities at the same time in the presence of manifold market failures. Moreover, comprehensive research of the impact of the policy measures on the participating households, is missing in the previous literatures. By incorporating the household model into technical efficiency analysis framework, household level technical efficiency analysis takes both on – farm and off – farm activities into account. This book, therefore, aims to shed some light on issues related to the impact of GfG on participating rural households' agricultural production and general household livelihoods, especially on the productivity and efficiency at the farm and farm – household level.

Using data collected from the rural households in the villages of several catchments from Ansai and Yanchang County, Shaanxi Province on the Loss Plateau of China, four empirical studies were carried out to fulfill the obligations. Considering the importance of agricultural production for food security and sustainable development in the target areas, both panel data analysis on agricultural total factor productivity change and cross – sectional analysis on farm efficiency were conducted using data envelopment analysis method in the first two empirical studies. Diversification of livelihoods, especially off – farm work and its income has steadily become a force to be recked with within the agenda of sustainable agricultural and rural livelihoods. An endogenous switching regression analysis was therefore taken in the following empirical study to examine the factors that influence household decisions to participate in off – farm work and estimate the impact of participation on productivity and other household welfare measures under the auspices of GfG. This method allows us to treat the observed heterogeneity of the off – farm participation decision that may confound its impacts on productivity and other household welfare measures. The last empirical study analyzed household level technical efficiency, considering both farm and off – farm activities simultaneously. This is of vital importance given the intricate relationship between farm and off – farm activities.

In general, the result reminds us the possible wealth effect of conservation payments, which serve as the critical policy measure of GfG. The wealth effect undermines the effectiveness of the program. Instead of compensating households for conserving sloping land, the implications suggest an alternative policy orientation that includes land consolidation; better childcare arrangements; education, training, extension services, and other human capital increasing initiatives; improved transportation infrastructure; and improving and facilitating access to land, labor, and credit markets for smallholders. This sheds new light on the most effective policy options to achieve the goals of sustainable agriculture and rural livelihoods of the households on the Loess Plateau. The result of the study has important implications for the next round of subsidy scheme which might start in few years.

The book is based on the author's PhD and postdoc research. It is funded by the Core University Program and Global Center of Excellence Program sponsored by Japan Society for the Promotion of Science, National Natural Science Foundation of China (No. 41701139) and the academic publication fund of Guangdong University of Finance and Economics. However, the findings, interpretations and conclusions expressed in this book are entirely those of the author's and should not be attributed to others, which does not guarantee their accuracy and can accept no responsibility for any consequences of their use. The author has endeavored to the work，but she is aware there are many drawbacks in terms of both content and grammar，then the author welcomes any suggestions and constructive criticism from readers. The author hopes the book would be useful in enriching the repertoire of knowledge.

·

Contents

◆ 退耕还林政策与黄土高原地区农户可持续生计：基于生产率和效率的实证研究
Grain for Green Program and Sustainable Agriculture and Rural Livelihoods of the Loess
Plateau in China：Empirical Studies with Measurement of Productivity and Efficiency

◇ 退耕还林政策与黄土高原地区农户可持续生计：基于生产率和效率的实证研究
Grain for Green Program and Sustainable Agriculture and Rural Livelihoods of the Loess
Plateau in China: Empirical Studies with Measurement of Productivity and Efficiency

Chapter 1　General Introduction

1. 1　Poverty – Environment Nexus in Less Favored Areas

Despite decades of government efforts, poverty eradication and environmental conservation in the less – favored rural areas remain among the greatest challenges facing many developing countries (Liu et al. , 2015). According to the latest report of the Secretary – General on the Implementation of the Third United Nations Decade for the Eradication of Poverty (2018 – 2027), an estimated 783 million people lived on extreme poverty (less than $ 1. 90 a day) in 2013, mostly in less – developed countries (The United Nations, 2018).

In the remote and less favored areas of the developing countries, subsistence farmers who depend on the environment and natural resources for food, fiber and fuel, which stained their carry capacity, have traditionally taken the brunt of the blame for the severe poverty and environmental degradation problems (Duraiappah, 1998). In the presence of imperfect markets and institutional failures which inhibit their participating in off – farm

◆ 退耕还林政策与黄土高原地区农户可持续生计：基于生产率和效率的实证研究
Grain for Green Program and Sustainable Agriculture and Rural Livelihoods of the Loess
Plateau in China: Empirical Studies with Measurement of Productivity and Efficiency

labor market or investing in land – productivity – enhancing agricultural practices, the small holder farmers were obliged to make inefficient allocation
choices, such as overcultivation and overgrazing, to satisfy the need of
growing population (Duraiappah, 1998; Grosjean and Kontoleon, 2009).
The consequences not only include on – site impact of escalating land degradation and perpetuated and intensified poverty along with the decline in land
fertility, but also off – site impact of water flood and dust storms.

As a result, economists pointed out that institutional factors might play
a large role in correcting these troublesome market failures, while simultaneously serve the purposes of both eradicating the prevalence of poverty and the
spread of environmental externalities, given the interlinked and mutually re-
inforcing nature of the problems (Grosjean and Kontoleon, 2009). Payment for ecosystem services (PES) programs, among others, are getting
more and more popularity in the past decades as a kind of policy intervention
to tackle the problems simultaneously, and the leading countries include
Mexico, Costa Rica and China (Wunder et al., 2008). Through this
kind of program, financial incentives were provided to those who "supply"
ecosystem services, including farmers who agree to set aside sensitive land
or adopt farming technologies that generate ecosystem services such as protection of watershed functions (Delang and Yuan, 2015). The conservation
payment contributes to increased household income directly and indirectly
through the liquidity effect on participating farm households. In this way, the
two objectives of environmental conservation and rural poverty alleviation are
achieved by the program, in effect killing two birds with one stone.

1. 2   Unsustainable Development on the Loess Plateau

The Loess Plateau, located in northwestern China, includes almost all of Shanxi, Shaanxi, Gansu, Qinghai and Henan provinces, the Ningxia Hui and the Inner Mongolia Autonomous Regions, and parts of others in the upper and middle of China's Yellow River, covers an area of around 0. 64 million km^2 (Wu et al. , 2004) and is home to over 69 million farmers. The area is one of the world – famous regions that is most critically affected by land degradation, especially soil erosion (Shi and Shao, 2000) . The annual soil loss due to soil water erosion reached $2000 - 2500$ t km^{-2} $year^{-1}$ in early 1990s (Shi and Shao, 2000) . The extreme susceptibility of the topsoil to wind and water erosion and the highly concentrated precipitation are partly responsible for the severe soil erosion. But the irrational agricultural practices, such as excess reclamation, deforestation and overgrazing, play a more important role (Shi and Shao, 2000; Ash and Edmonds, 1998) . Last half century, however, as a result of rapidly increasing population and other political and socio – economic factors, the Loess Plateau presented an accelerating trend toward land reclamation, overgrazing and deforestation, even on marginal land and sloping land, which exacerbates land degradation. Lin and Ho (2003) estimated that over 70 million hectares of barren land, pasture, or forest was reclaimed up to 1996, mainly in the western interior and northern frontiers where there were fragile environments. The study by Ash and Edmonds (1998) reported that the degraded land accounted for 71. 30% of cultivated areas on the Loess Plateau in the

◇ 退耕还林政策与黄土高原地区农户可持续生计：基于生产率和效率的实证研究

Grain for Green Program and Sustainable Agriculture and Rural Livelihoods of the Loess Plateau in China：Empirical Studies with Measurement of Productivity and Efficiency

early 1990s.

The direct consequence of land degradation, as can be judged by the definition, is the decline in land productivity, or more precisely, "the loss of land productivity, quantitatively or qualitatively through various processes such as wind and soil erosion, salinization, waterlogging, and depletion of soil nutrients and soil contaminants" (Taddese, 2001). According to a national survey conducted at the 287 counties and municipalities in 1985, average grain yields on the Loess Plateau were 298 kg per mu (1.0 mu = 0.067 hectare) compared with a national average of 364 kg per mu, the more low – yielding land among which were on the eroded hilly land (Huang and Zhang, 1989). Land degradation may also have important negative externalities effects and result in an overall loss of other vital ecosystem services. Examples include the deposition of eroded soil in down – streams which increases the incidence and severity of flooding and droughts, and healthy threat or property damage by sand – storms as a result of floating wind – eroded dust. In 1997, severe droughts occurred along the middle to lower reaches of the Yellow River, and the river – bed of the latter dried up for 267 days; in 1998, massive floods spread over the Yangtze River and waterways in the northeast, claimed thousands' lives and caused massive damages (Uchida et al., 2005).

1.3　The Launch of the Grain for Green Program

In response to the unsustainable development on the Loess Plateau and other soil eroded regions, the Chinese government initiated a Paying for Environmental Services program—the Grain for Green (GfG) program to commit to prohibit the unsustainable agricultural practices, contributing both eco – environmental reclamation and poverty alleviation problems. This program is also known as Sloping Land Conversion Program (SLCP).

In August 1999, during a visit to Shaanxi, Zhu Rongji, the Premier of the P. R. C. then, articulated the intention of land retirement, as the beginning of the conversion program. The pilot project was first launched on three western provinces of Shaanxi, Sichuan, and Gansu, the areas with the most severe land degradation (mainly located at the middle and upper reaches of the Yellow River Basin and upper reaches of the Yangtze River Basin). The key measure of the project was to "sign contract with peasants who volunteer to set aside steep cropland or low – yield marginal land for forest and grassland, keep and build the vegetation, while the government compensate them with grain, cash or tree seedlings" (State Council of the P. R. C. , 1999). As the pilot project was reported to gain widespread acclaim, the government expanded the project to 17 provinces and districts in 2000 (with the other 14 provinces being Beijing, Chongqing, Guizhou, Hebei, Heilongjiang, Henan, Hubei, Hunan, Inner Mongolia, Jilin, Liaoning, Ningxia, Qinghai and Shanxi), along the middle and upper reaches of the Yellow River Basin and upper reaches of the Yangtze River Basin (SFA, MOLAR and SMF, 2000). In 2002, the government announced the official launch of the Project to cover 25 provinces (with the other 8 provinces being Anhui, Guangxi, Hainan, Jiangxi, Tianjin, Tibet, Xinjiang and Yunnan, including 1897 counties altogether), involving 73. 91% of the national land (State Council of the P. R. C. , 2002). They included GfG part of the Tenth Five – Year Plan officially and declared their intention to

◇ 退耕还林政策与黄土高原地区农户可持续生计：基于生产率和效率的实证研究
Grain for Green Program and Sustainable Agriculture and Rural Livelihoods of the Loess
Plateau in China: Empirical Studies with Measurement of Productivity and Efficiency

convert 34 million mu of marginal croplands on steep hillsides and slopes, together with 39. 93 million mu of waste land and mountains, to grassland and forests during the next 10 years (2002 – 2011) .

As the principal measure in the program, the government provides subsidy in the form of grain, cash and seedlings with different standard based on the judgment of different areas and different practices. For the converted farmland in the Yangtze River Basin or southern region, 150 kg of grain (or cash with equivalent value) were subsidized annually per mu as compensation; and for those in the Yellow River Basin and northern region, 100 kg of grain (or cash equivalent) were subsidized annually per mu. And for both regions, 20 yuan (1 yuan = 0. 133 USD, as of 2007) per mu were provided as living subsidy. The duration of the subsidies was enacted to be eight years for converting farmland into ecological forest, five years for economic forest and two years for grassland, whereas ecological forest refers to forest with trees which have significant ecological functions, and economic forest refers to forest with trees which produce marketable crop, other than timber (usually fruit or nuts) . Subsidies for seeds and seedlings as well as cost in afforestation are provided 50 yuan per mu by the central government in one lump sum. Since subsidy alone does not guarantee longer – term livelihoods mechanism and success of the program, the government in 2005 announced to supplement with some side – measures to help foster longer term livelihoods (State Council of the P. R. C. , 2005) . They include "farmland improvement (or the construction of basic farmland); rural energy; emigration; livelihood diversification; mountain enclosure, pasture prohibition, and captive breeding to protect the achievements made in conversion of farmland to forest", etc. Whereas the aims and main guidelines of the program are set by central government at a national level, the implementation is at the provincial level.

　　The first phase of the program lasted eight years and ended in 2007. Subsequent efforts have been devoted to consolidating the achievements on formerly cultivated sloping land by reforestation and resettlement (State Council of the P. R. C. , 2007) . In addition to continued subsidy, special fund is established to foster long – term livelihoods, primarily used on farmland construction, rural energy popularization, emigration and afforestation in the central and western areas (State Council of the P. R. C. , 2007) . Due to the strong desire of local government and rural households, the Chinese government declared its intention firstly in 2014 to enlarge the scale of land conversion by another 42. 4 million mu (P. R. C. , 2015) and later altered to 80 million mu in 2017, to compensate the farmers for an additional five years. The central government paid 2000 yuan altogether for planting trees and 1000 yuan for planting grasses. At the meantime, the central government also delegated the authority over the decision of the subsidy standard to provincial administrations, in the case that they were willing and able to subsidize more with local budgets (P. R. C. , 2015; State Council of the P. R. C. , 2016) . It is noticeable that GfG has been incorporated into the Protection and Restoration of the Forest Eco – system Fund in 2018 (SFA and NFGA, 2018) . Refer to Table 1 – 1 for the timeline of GfG policies and implementations.

Table 1 – 1　Historical Milestones of GfG

Year	Milestone
1999	Pilot projects started in Sichuan, Shaanxi and Gansu Provinces
2000	GfG is officially a significant part of the Great Western Development Strategy started in more provinces (altogether 17 provinces); Relevant principles and policies are formulated

续表

Year	Milestone
2002	Nationwide official launch of GfG（involving 25 provinces）
2007	GfG subsidy scheme renewed for another round
2014	GfG subsidy scheme renewed and the scale substantially enlarged（involving 22 provinces and Xinjiang Production and Construction Corps）
2018	GfG is incorporated into the Protection and Restoration of the Forest Eco – system Fund

1. 4　Literature Review on GfG

By the middle of 2019, over 500 million mu of marginal or sloping lands had been reforested, affecting 32 million rural households, with an expenditure of over 5 hundred billion Chinese Yuan（P. R. C. , 2019）.

Given the large operating scale, huge public investment, and profound environment and well – being implications, broad attention had been drawn from academic circles domestically and abroad. Unsurprisingly, many studies have focused on the effectiveness and impact of the program in environmental rehabilitation, economic development, and poverty alleviation（refer to Delang and Yuan, 2015 for a review of relevant studies）. Most studies concur that the ecological consequences of GfG have been positive, especially in relation to soil fertility and the improvement of soil conditions. Soil erosion and river sedimentation have slowed down. Through planting ecological trees, the program also contributed considerably to carbon sequestration（Delang and Yuan, 2015）. According to McVicar et al. （2002）, some 150, 000 km^2 of eroded land has been controlled by various conservation measures. The flow of sediments into the Yellow River has been reduced by about 300 million tons/year.

Nevertheless, this book is more concerned with its economic implications. Actually, as a payment for ecosystem services program, the payments are provided by the government, which means they are made for a fixed term due to budget constraints. Unless farm householders are able to shift their agricultural practices and other income – generating – activities with the relaxation of their liquidity constraints to generate sustainable livelihoods, the programs won't succeed (Wunder et al. , 2008; Grosjean and Kontoleon, 2009; Uchida et al. , 2009), regardless of the environmental benefits they brought. Because there are chances that the farmers would refrain from reclamation if the subsidies were to be ceased. In addition, for a farmland set – aside program like GfG in China, there is a major concern that the loss of cultivated land area might lead to a decrease in agricultural production that will threaten food security and social stability and thus condemn any follow – up investment and irrevocably stymie the program (Feng et al. , 2005; Deng et al. , 2006; Sun et al. , 2006; Uchida et al. , 2007; Xu et al. , 2006a; Xu et al. , 2006b) . It is therefore reasonable that the sustainability or success of the program is widely acknowledged to be dependent upon its ability to improve agricultural productivity or to enable households to access alternative employment opportunities (Xu et al. , 2004; Uchida et al. , 2007; Xu et al. , 2010) . Households are less likely to cultivate sloping land, which has a much lower marginal productivity of labor, if the output of the remaining farmland improves (Deng et al. , 2006) or they have access to more attractive off – farm jobs (Groom et al. , 2010) so that the improved income can offset the loss of agricultural output from the set – aside

◇ 退耕还林政策与黄土高原地区农户可持续生计：基于生产率和效率的实证研究
Grain for Green Program and Sustainable Agriculture and Rural Livelihoods of the Loess
Plateau in China: Empirical Studies with Measurement of Productivity and Efficiency

land. Therefore, the literature review focuses especially on the agricultural production and diversified livelihoods of participating farmers. This has important policy implications on the program and its sustainability.

1.4.1 Impact Analysis of GfG on Agricultural Production and Rural Livelihoods

Many previous studies have been devoted to the impact of GfG on participating households' agricultural production (e. g. , Feng et al. , 2005) and their labor reallocation to more profitable activities, especially on off – farm employment (Peng et al. , 2007; Uchida et al. , 2007; Uchida et al. , 2009; Yao et al. , 2010; Yin et al. , 2014; Zhen et al. , 2014). The majority of the research finds a shift of the labor force toward off – farm employment (e. g. , Uchida et al. , 2009; Groom et al. , 2010; Yao et al. , 2010; Kelly and Huo, 2013; Yin et al. , 2014; Zhen et al. , 2014), which may contribute to improved household income or wellbeing; however, the impact on agricultural production has received less attention and the result is less clear. Xie et al. (2006) and Yao et al. (2010) found evidence of improved land use intensity or agricultural investments, which might contribute to improved agricultural production, while others show different results (Feng et al. , 2005; Xu et al. , 2006; Cheng and Liu, 2007; Cheng et al. , 2010; Zhen et al. , 2014). Actually, there is always the debate over the competence or complimentary relationship between farm and off – farm activities. Generally speaking, off – farm employment may contribute to farm household welfare by providing another source of income (Holden et al. , 2004), and therefore relax farmers' liquidity constraint and enable farmers to make productivity – enhancing investments

(Oseni and Winters, 2009; Pfeiffer et al. , 2009). But the liquidity re-laxation effect occurs only when the farm household faces liquidity con-straints and capital from other sources is not available. When the farmer household faces imperfections in the markets, off – farm employment may compete with farm production for labor and other resources, leading to a de-crease in agricultural production (Reardon et al. , 1994; Pfeiffer et al. , 2009). The situation is even worse in the developing countries where the family members participating in off – farm work are generally physically stronger and have a higher educational attainment (Rozelle et al. , 1999). The labor loss would lead to a decrease in agricultural productivity with changes in household human capital (Shi, 2018). In these cases, the contribution of off – farm employment to household welfare might be compro-mised. Unless the contribution of off – farm income to household income out-weighs the lost – labor and capital effect, off – farm employment won't con-tribute to increased household welfare.

Many studies examined the impact on household welfare directly. With different case study areas, most of the studies came to the same conclusion that the program has greatly increased farmers' income, and contributed to the sustainability and stability of the local society (Liu, 1999; Xu et al. , 2004; Liu et al, 2005; Feng et al. , 2005; Peng et al. , 2007; Uchida et al. , 2007; Wang et al. , 2007; Xu et al, 2006a; Zhou et al. , 2007; Cao et al. , 2009; Zhou et al. , 2009; Komarek et al. , 2014, to mention a few). However, this would not be the case if conservation payments from the program were withdrawn (Xu et al. , 2004; Wang et al. , 2007). Most of these studies based their conclusions on a simple comparison of household income before and after participation, or on a comparison of in-

◇ 退耕还林政策与黄土高原地区农户可持续生计：基于生产率和效率的实证研究
Grain for Green Program and Sustainable Agriculture and Rural Livelihoods of the Loess
Plateau in China：Empirical Studies with Measurement of Productivity and Efficiency

come from participants and non – participants. However, these differences might originate from unobserved heterogeneity. For example, households participating in the program or in off – farm employment might have characteristics quite different from those of non – participants. And other times, increase in household income (subsidy excluded) before and after the program might be due to economic development itself. Comparison of the difference in income between participants and non – participants is unreliable, too, which might originate from some unobserved heterogeneity between participating and non – participating groups. Uchida et al. (2005) and Xu et al. (2004), both using standard program evaluation methodologies, on the other hand, found impact on household per capita income insignificant with field survey data conducted in 2003.

The effectiveness of the program on the livelihoods of the participating households requires a more nuanced understanding of the poor households that it targets (Groom et al., 2010). However, some previous studies have criticized the targeting of the program design for showing no predominant targeting on poorer households or environmentally sensitive plots, and no incentive for post – program land use decisions of the participating farmers to land conservation thus compromised the sustainability of the program (Uchida et al., 2005; Xu et al., 2004).

1.4.2 Mechanism of the Impact of GfG on Agricultural Production and Rural Livelihoods

As indicated in section 1.3.1, the majority of the research finds that agricultural practices were moving from subsistence farming towards more intensive higher – return cash crops (Xie et al., 2006; Uchida et al.,

2009), and increased capital inputs (Yao et al. , 2010), and the labor force was shifting towards off – farm employment (Uchida et al. , 2009; Groom et al. , 2010; Yao et al. , 2010; Kelly and Huo, 2013; Yin et al. , 2014; Zhen et al. , 2014) . This has been explained by the liquidity effect of the conservation payments. However, some other researchers have found evidence that the effectiveness of government conservation payments on the efficient reallocation of household labor to other activities, and on the more efficient utilization of capital resources is less clear (Xue, 2007; Liang et al. , 2012) . Uchida et al. (2007) proposed a framework showing that the impact of a land retirement program like GfG on the reallocation of labor should be a trade – off between the substitution effect and the wealth effect. In the former case, households shift labor freed by the program to more productive activities, i. e. , off – farm employment, while in the latter case', the subsidy income would discourage farmers from both farm and off – farm work. The notion of the wealth effect was firstly developed by Donnellan and Hennessy (2012) . They propose that decoupled subsidy (payments that are irrelevant to current production or price) may induce a wealth effect that allows farmers to work less while maintaining consumption levels. The wealth effect has been widely tested and verified in empirical studies of decoupled subsidies (e. g. , Ahearn et al. , 2006; El – Osta et al. , 2008; Bojnec and Latruffe, 2013) . Even though conservation payments resemble the characteristics of decoupled subsidy, the wealth effect is generally of less concern under GfG. The conspicuous exception is found the work of Liang et al. (2012), which claimed to find a negative relationship between subsidies and on – farm and off – farm income.

◇ 退耕还林政策与黄土高原地区农户可持续生计：基于生产率和效率的实证研究
Grain for Green Program and Sustainable Agriculture and Rural Livelihoods of the Loess
Plateau in China： Empirical Studies with Measurement of Productivity and Efficiency

1. 5   Objectives of the Book

To sum up with previous studies, it remains uncertain whether the program, with conservation payments as its major measure, has really improved agricultural production, promoted off – farm employment participation, and contributed to sustainable livelihoods of the participating farmers. If not, how should policies be adjusted to better facilitate agricultural production, off – farm employment and improve household welfare and sustainable livelihoods?

Given the fact that productivity and efficiency play a key role in agricultural production and rural livelihoods, yet previous researches had seldom systematically studied the households participating in the program on their productivity improvement and efficiency aspect, this book aims to contribute to literatures from a productivity and efficiency perspective. Under the new framework of program, subsidy standards vary between regions because regional governments were empowered to set local subsidy standards, this book will pay special attention to the impact of the amount of the subsidy. The parameters have practical importance because the current round of payment would end in the following one or two years (The State Council of the P. R. C. , 2016) and new operation mechanisms might be introduced in the near future according to the Regulations on the Protection and Restoration of the Forest Ecosystem Fund (SFA and NFGA, 2018) .

This book thus aimed at contributing to the literatures, with an understanding of how GfG affected the participating rural households' agricultural production and general household livelihoods, especially on the productivity and efficiency at the farm and farm – household level. Specifically, the book would like to focus on the following questions:

(1) It is justified to be cautious about the possible decrease in agricultural production with the loss of cultivated land area which might threaten food security and social stability. Total Factor Productivity (TFP, measured as the ratio of aggregate output to aggregate input) and Technical Efficiency (TE, measured as the actual output to the ideal output) play a key role in agricultural production. In context of land retirement program, increase in TFP and TE would contribute to total agricultural production that would offset or even outweigh the production loss resulting from the loss of arable land. We are therefore concerned that what changes has been induced by the program on TFP and TE of the participating farms for the agricultural production? And how efficient are the farms' agricultural production under the prevailing circumstances, including the emerging technology and shrinkage of land area, etc. , brought about by the program? What factors contributed to improved TFP and increased efficiencies?

(2) Diversified livelihoods, especially off – farm activities, rather than relying only on subsistence farming are generally thought as a strategy that enables households to improve their incomes, increase agricultural production, and enhance food security by smoothing capital constraints. Therefore, it is essential to study the impact of the program on off – farm employment and household welfare. Due to the intricate relationship between off – farm activities and farm activities in the developing countries (De Janvry and Sadoulet, 2006), however, the impact of off – farm employment on household welfare should be studied carefully. Farm household level techni-

◇ 退耕还林政策与黄土高原地区农户可持续生计：基于生产率和效率的实证研究
Grain for Green Program and Sustainable Agriculture and Rural Livelihoods of the Loess
Plateau in China：Empirical Studies with Measurement of Productivity and Efficiency

cal efficiency is a new notion （Chavas et al. , 2005） that extending traditional technical efficiency analysis at the farm level to the household level,
which taking farm production and off – farm income generation into consideration simultaneously. In the setting of a land set – aside program like GfG， a
household level technical efficiency analysis provides important information
on the performance of the households' utilization of its available technology
and resources （including labor， capital and the remaining farm land,
etc. ） to maximize its household income， therefore is indicative of the sustainability of its livelihoods （Scoones， 1998） . We therefore would like to
give a farm – household technical efficiency analysis and find out its determinant factors.

This will be done through four empirical studies：

（1） By using Data – Envelopment – Analysis based Malmquist Index
analysis on sample household data from the Loess Plateau， the TFP change
before and after the implementation of the program， at a farm level （inclu-
ding variables only for agricultural production）， would be generated. The index can be decomposed into technological growth and changes in technical
efficiency， and the latter of which can be further decomposed into changes
in pure technical efficiency and changes in allocative efficiency. Then a regression analysis will be taken to simulate the relationship of the explanatory
variables and the dependent variables — the changes in TFP and its components. The farm or farm – household specific socio – economic characters and
other variables， such as the measures of the program， are included as explanatory variables to simulate its impact on changes in TFP and its components.

（2） By using data envelopment analysis method， the efficiencies of the participant farm – households on agricultural production under the new technology will be estimated. Economic efficiency (or cost efficiency in this book) can be decomposed into allocative efficiency and technical efficiency, while technical efficiency can be decomposed into pure technical efficiency and scale efficiency. The structures and properties of the efficiencies will be revealed. And the farm and farm – household specific socio – economic characters and other variables, such as the measures of the program, will be taken for a regression analysis to find out the determinant factors for inefficiencies.

(3) Employing endogenous switching regression method which accounts for the unobserved endogeneity of the off – farm participation decision that may confound its impacts on household welfare, empirical study is conducted to examine the factors that influence household decisions to participate in off – farm work and estimate the impact of participation on household welfare under the auspices of GfG.

(4) Due to the intricate relationship of off – farm activities on farm activities, we introduce the farm – household model, which captures both farm and off – farm activities simultaneously, to be incorporated with data envelopment analysis method to estimate the farm – household level efficiency. And then a regression analysis will be taken to find out the factors determine farm – household efficiency.

The data collection process was a joint effort between Arid Land Research Center, Tottori University in Japan and the Institute of Soil and Water Conservation, Chinese Academy of Sciences. The institute, located in Shaanxi Province on the Loess Plateau, has focused all its attention on the environmental and economic problems of the Loess Plateau for decades

◇ 退耕还林政策与黄土高原地区农户可持续生计：基于生产率和效率的实证研究
Grain for Green Program and Sustainable Agriculture and Rural Livelihoods of the Loess
Plateau in China：Empirical Studies with Measurement of Productivity and Efficiency

(Tsunekawa et al., 2014) and the research group has done field surveys and randomly collected data annually since 1980s. As suggested by a senior researcher from the institute, we firstly selected Zhifanggou, Xiannangou and Danangou in Ansai County as the study area. The institute provided sample data collected in this area in 1999 for our panel data analysis. We paid two visits (May of 2008 and September to October of 2008) on our own to collect data in 2007, the ending year of the first phase. The sampling was mainly based on the randomly collected sample data in 1999. The questionnaire includes all data related to household demographics, asset holdings, source of income, use of labor and cost of other inputs, details of participation in the program, the agricultural production and other activities for all the household members. Altogether 112 samples were finally deemed as valid (samples with abnormal values and missing values were excluded). Realizing the limitation of the sample size, a supplementary investigation was taken in September to October of 2009 with the main objective of expanding the sample size. According to suggestions from local supervision office, catchments from Yanchang Counties (including Guoqigou and Liyongbian catchments), with similar natural, economic, social conditions and agronomic practices, were selected. About 1/5 of the permanent residents from the catchments were randomly selected for detailed face – to – face interviews using structured questionnaires. Altogether we got 225 valid samples.

1.6 Organization of the Book

The book is composed of eight chapters which are separated as follows：

In Chapter 1, an overview of the background of the Loess Plateau and GfG, the existing literatures with regards to the impact and sustainability analysis of the program is given. The intention and the goal of the study followed by the structure used are also specified in this Chapter.

The significance of analyzing the productivity and efficiency of the farm and farm households participating in the program for the benefit of sustainable agriculture and rural livelihoods in the study areas are expounded in Chapter 2.

Chapter 3 introduced the study areas.

Chapter 4 concentrates on the farm total factor productivity, technology and technical efficiency change induced by the program, and its determinant factors.

Chapter 5 concentrates on the farm technical efficiency, allocative efficiency and scale efficiency of the households and its determinant factors.

Chapter 6 concentrates on the factors influence decisions to participate in off – farm work and estimate the impact of participation on household welfare.

Chapter 7 concentrates on the farm – household technical efficiency and its determinant factors.

Chapter 8 attempts to synthesize the outcomes got from the four case studies described in previous chapters, discuss the findings in a broader context, draw conclusions from the work, The limitations of the book and highlight for further directions for future research is also given.

Chapter 2　Justification of Productivity, Efficiency Analysis under the Context of GfG

Factor (or resource) scarcity and thus the need for resources – saving and environmentally friendly practices is the major impetus for the increasing interest in efficiency and productivity studies. Both efficiency and productivity are indicators to reflect the performance of the producer (or decision – making – unit, DMU). These two indicators are closely related and often appear together in the literature, even though their meanings are divergent (as shown in section 2.1 and 2.2, respectively). While the ultimate goals of GfG are to realize sustainable agriculture and rural livelihoods of the participating households and sustainable development in the ecologically fragile areas, the analysis of productivity and efficiency issues at the farm and household level is of vital importance under the context of GfG.

2.1　Productivity and Efficiency

2.1.1　Productivity

By the *productivity* of a producer, we mean the ratio of the amount of output produced to the amounts of inputs used. According to the resources we take into consideration, productivity measures can be subdivided into either partial or total measures.

Partial productivity is the amount of output per unit of a particular input. Commonly used partial measures include yield (output per unit of land), and labor productivity (output per labor force, either per person or per agricultural person – hour) . Both measures can be used to reflect rural welfare or living standards since it reflects the ability to acquire income through sale of agricultural goods or agricultural production. Partial measures of productivity can be misleading or sometimes hard to distinguish their implications, especially in the case of several inputs. For example, two farms may have the same labor productivity, but their land productivity may differ greatly.

To take account for the problems with partial productivity, the multi – factor productivity, also called as total factor productivity (TFP) , was proposed. TFP is the ratio of an index of agricultural output to an index of agricultural inputs. The index of agricultural output is a value – weighted sum of all agricultural production components. The index of agricultural inputs is the value – weighted sum of agricultural inputs. Conventionally, the inputs include land, labor, physical capital, young livestock and chemical fertilizers and pesticides. Growth in TFP is referred to as the Solow residual. Solow introduced in his sequential work in 1956 and 1957, an unobservable residual to the production function relation (the relation between the growth and the accumulation of physical capital like investment in industries and infrastructure) , which he interpreted as exogenously evolving technical progress or, more simply, technology (Solow, 1956; Solow, 1957) . Jorgenson

◇ 退耕还林政策与黄土高原地区农户可持续生计：基于生产率和效率的实证研究
Grain for Green Program and Sustainable Agriculture and Rural Livelihoods of the Loess
Plateau in China: Empirical Studies with Measurement of Productivity and Efficiency

and Griliches （1967） had given a more precise definition that change in TFP is the difference between the rate of growth of real product and the rate of growth of real factor input. Growth in TFP is generally considered as a measure of technological progress that can be attributed to changes in agricultural research and development （R&D）, extension services, human capital development such as education and physical, commercial infrastructure, as well as government policies and environmental degradation （Ahearn et al. , 1998）. Change in TFP can also be due to unmeasured inputs or imperfectly measured inputs.

2. 1. 2　Efficiency

By definition of *efficiency* of a producer, we mean a comparison of the observed DMU against the optimal value （frontier）. The theoretical framework underlying efficiency analysis dates to the work of Koopmans （1951）, Debreu （1951）, and Farrell （1957）, who made the first attempt at empirical estimation of efficiencies for a set of observed production units. A presence of inefficiency can be attributed to differences in production technology, differences in the scale of operation, differences in operating efficiency and differences in the operating environment in which production occurs （Fried et al. , 2008）. It is a measure that enables the management to gain information about the inefficiency （Leibenstein, 1966） referred to the production process of any unit, which may be influenced by economic factors internal to any firm （differences in production technology, differences in the scale of operation, differences in operating efficiency） and other factors not tightly under the control of the management （differences in the operating environment）.

Efficiency can be either classified into output – oriented (or output orientation) and input – orientated (or input orientation). The former refers to the ability to avoid waste by producing as much output as possible as input usage allows, and the latter means by using as little input as output production allows. Farrell (1957) decomposed economic efficiency—the ability of a DMU to get more output at minimum cost, into two components, given the assumption of constant returns – to – scale (CRS). One component is technical efficiency. The other is allocative efficiency (termed as price efficiency by Farrell, 1957), which refers to the ability to combine inputs and outputs in optimal proportions in light of prevailing prices. Since technical efficiency as defined above takes no account of the scale effect, Banker et al. (1984) introduced the concept of technical efficiency under the assumption of variable returns – to – scale (VRS), which was later called pure technical efficiency, to distinguish scale efficiency from technical efficiency. Scale efficiency measures whether the DMU is operating at the optimal size at which change in size will not improve output or revenue.

2.2   Sustainable Agriculture and Rural Livelihoods

The word "sustainable", is defined as "*causing little or no damage to the environment and therefore able to continue for a long time*" (*Cambridge Advanced Learners' Dictionary*). There is little disagreement on the definition of "sustainable", but when it refers to "sustainable development", there is no universal and unequivocal definition of this word. Even though the concept was popularized by World Commission on Environment and Develop-

◇ 退耕还林政策与黄土高原地区农户可持续生计：基于生产率和效率的实证研究
Grain for Green Program and Sustainable Agriculture and Rural Livelihoods of the Loess
Plateau in China: Empirical Studies with Measurement of Productivity and Efficiency

ment (WECD), as "*sustainable development is development that meets the needs of the present without compromising the ability of future generations to meet their own needs*" (WECD, 1987). The concept should be operationalized in case – specific and interdisciplinary definitions, taking into account the social, economic and environmental objectives of various stakeholders involved (Lopez et al., 2006). The sustainable development within a rural context, also involves massive divergent understandings using different terms, based on different priorities. The most common ones, stressing the sustainability within the rural context, include "sustainable agriculture", "sustainable farming", "sustainable agriculture and rural development", and "sustainable agriculture and rural livelihoods". Even though rural society is principally involved in agriculture – related activities, especially in the developing countries, agriculture, however, is only one element of a range of interlinked strategies to sustain rural livelihoods. Non – farm activities are growing in importance in the developing world for the lives of the rural poor. Recognising the interlinked strategies, the theme of agriculture and rural livelihoods adopts a holistic view in supporting rural livelihoods, considering the full range of livelihood options that can support people. The wording of sustainable agriculture and rural livelihoods is given from a more subtle level, sustainable agriculture and rural development (SARD) is more commonly used and given from a macro – level. Food and Agriculture Organisation (FAO, 1991) of the United Nations has given a definition of SARD, attempting to address environmental, economic, social and technical dimensions of food production and rural development altogether, which is given as follows:

"*The management and conservation of the natural resource base, and the orientation of technological and institutional change in such a manner as to ensure the attainment and continued satisfaction of human needs for present and future generations. Such development conserves land, water, plant genetic resources, is environmentally non − degrading, technologically appropriate, economically viable and socially acceptable"* (FAO, 1991).

This definition has been refined and ratified as the *Action Plan for Sustainable Development* (also known as *Chapter* 14 *of Agenda* 21) adopted by the United Nations Conference on Environment and Development (UNCED, 1992), which has been endorsed by 178 governments. The objective of SARD has been stated to be related with:

"①*food security, by ensuring an appropriate and sustainable balance between self − sufficiency and self − reliance*; ②*employment and income generation in rural areas, particularly to eradicate poverty*; ③*natural resource conservation and environmental protection.*"

To propose a more precise definition of sustainable development in the rural area that would be generally accepted by all intellectuals and stakeholders might be infeasible. Despite the variation in the wording, however, we can judge from the definition and SARD related policy agenda that livelihoods perspectives, including that of farm production and off − farm activities, is central to SARD thinking and practice; and the central theme contained in most definitions is on improving or maintaining output while maintaining or enhancing the quality and regenerative potential of natural resources.

◇ 退耕还林政策与黄土高原地区农户可持续生计：基于生产率和效率的实证研究
Grain for Green Program and Sustainable Agriculture and Rural Livelihoods of the Loess
Plateau in China： Empirical Studies with Measurement of Productivity and Efficiency

2. 3　Justification of Productivity and Efficiency Analysis under the Context of GfG for the Sake of Sustainable Agriculture and Rural Livelihoods

Actually, earlier use of the term "sustainability" in ecological and agricultural literatures was exactly used in the context of "productivity", even though had hardly been noted outside the scientific community directly involved (Becker, 1997). The first effort stressed the importance of productivity to sustainability within an agroecosystem in the intellectual works might be attributed to Conway (1983), which had been refined later by himself in other works (Conway, 1987). He classifies the agroecosystems into the cropping system (plot level), farming/household system (farm level and farm – household level, the former of which generally include environment related to crop and livestock; the latter of which includes off – farm employment and trading, etc.), watershed/village (local level), and landscape/district (regional level) (Conway, 1997). As higher levels (national, supranational, and global) influence agriculture more indirectly by policy decisions or large – scale environmental changes (e. g. , acid rain or global warming), the agroecosystems in higher level are less referred to and more difficult to study. He claimed that： *"Sustainability is the ability of a system to maintain productivity in spite of a major disturbance, such as is caused by intensive stress or a large perturbation. "* The example of significant stress or perturbation, he suggests, might be a rare drought or flood, or new pest. He then brought forward the idea that "lack of sustainability may be indicated by declining productivity", but he also observed that when faced with major disturbance, "collapse may come suddenly and without warning," therefore "satisfactory methods of measuring sustainability still need to be found". Despite the authors' clarification, this interpretation has been widely accepted for sustainability assessment of agricultural systems (Barbier, 1987; Reardon, 1998). Tisdell (1988) has illustrated an outlook on Conway's (1983, 1987) criteria for assessing the desirability (sustainability) of agricultural systems. He maintains that the approach "involves several unresolved conceptual issues". But he also admitted that the preference of less developed countries should be on the sustainable productive systems (or maintenance of productivity). Other influential studies that stressed the importance of productivity include: Plucknett and Smith (1986), who suggested that effort should be steer toward "sustaining productivity and damping oscillations in crop and livestock yields" for the benefit of sustainable agriculture; and Lewandowski et al. (1999), who asserted that maintenance of productivity plays a key role in agricultural sustainability. In an overview article, Ruttan (1994) had observed that, "prior to the beginning of this century almost all increases in food production were obtained by bringing new land into production. By the first decades of the next century almost all increases in food production must come from higher yields", or from increased productivity.

A more recent work by Lynam and Herdt (1989), who advocated using the trend in TFP change as a significant measure for sustainability at a farm scale, takes the "sustainability—productivity" problem back to the focus of debate. He proposed that "... the appropriate measure of output by which to determine sustainability... is total factor productivity... ; a sus-

◇ 退耕还林政策与黄土高原地区农户可持续生计：基于生产率和效率的实证研究
Grain for Green Program and Sustainable Agriculture and Rural Livelihoods of the Loess
Plateau in China: Empirical Studies with Measurement of Productivity and Efficiency

tainable system has a non – negative trend in total factor productivity over the
period of concern". The premise behind this proposition might be related to
the understanding of sustainability in a way that maintains the agricultural
system over time in productivity, without degradation of the environment. A
non – negative TFP growth implies that output is increasing at least as fast as
inputs.

The application of the non – negative trend in TFP has been widely accepted among agronomists and others, as a measure of specific sustainable
agricultural system (for example, Ehui and Spencer, 1993; Murgai
et al., 2001; Tiongco and Dawe, 2002; Martinez – Cordero and Leung,
2004).

As two important impetuses for TFP growth, technological growth and
efficiency increase, their importance has also been realized (for example,
Altieri, 1989; Becker, 1997; Weitzman 1997; Callens and Tyteca,
1999; DeKoeijer et al., 2002; Clark and Dickson, 2003; Abay et al.,
2004; Vollebergh and Kemfert, 2005). There are some others (e. g.,
Barbier et al., 1990; Bishop, 1993) suggested that efficiency itself might
not be necessarily sufficient for sustainability, especially for a regional or
larger scale, but they all agreed that it is necessary to be efficient in order to
achieve sustainability.

The goal of GfG is to achieve sustainable agriculture and rural livelihoods for the participating households and sustainable development in the
target areas, and the major challenge is food security, poverty alleviation
and land conservation. It is therefore more significant to study from a productivity and efficiency issues from the farm and farm – household level to un-
derstand the effect of the program and the important parameters.

Chapter 3　General Description of the Study Area

Zhifanggou, Xiannangou and Danangou catchments (latitude 36°51′N, longitude 109°19′E) in the Ansai County and Guoqigou and Liyongbian catchments in Yanchang County, Shaanxi Province on the Loess Plateau was selected as the study area. The area lies in the hinterlands of the Loess Plateau and is characterized by typical hilly and gully areas with an altitude of 1010 – 1431m above sea level. Climatically, it belongs to a warm temperate zone with a semiarid continental climate with an average annual air temperature of 8.8℃, and an average annual precipitation of 535 mm (Guo et al., 2008). Rainfall shows high seasonal variability with about 75% falling from June to September, and high rainfall intensity always in the form of heavy rain (Jiao et al., 2008). As the degree of slope varies from 0° to 65° and the soils developed on wind – accumulated loess parent material, are very susceptible to erosion due to poor vegetation, rainfall is a principle extrinsic factor leading to soil erosion in the catchments. On vegetation regionalization, it was classified as forest – steppe area. Due to long – term human activity, most natural vegetation has been destroyed. Land use types include cropland, woodland, grassland, shrubland, orchards, and residential areas in a mosaic rural landscape pattern. Economically, agricultural produc-

◇ 退耕还林政策与黄土高原地区农户可持续生计：基于生产率和效率的实证研究
Grain for Green Program and Sustainable Agriculture and Rural Livelihoods of the Loess
Plateau in China: Empirical Studies with Measurement of Productivity and Efficiency

tion plays a crucial role in local economy, and the major crops are potatoes, beans, maize, millet and corns. But due to the feature of semi – arid continental climate, agriculture production in the study area is primarily rain – fed and prone to drought affection. Such as recorded in Dai et al. (2007), with poor vegetation and a typical semi – arid continental climate, the watershed has been pervaded by soil erosion, and grain yield was only about 25 kg/mu in the 1970s. Thus the subsistence farmers were among the poorest in China. With population growth and economic development, by the early 1990s the ratio of land under cultivation had increased to 47.9%, most of which were sloping land, and goat numbers had increased by half (Dai et al., 2007).

To avert the unsustainable agricultural practices, prevent land degradation and alleviate poverty, GfG was initiated in 1999 with some pilot projects. Both catchments were among the pilot areas and thus have been subjected to many program – sponsored measures with effective administration. Farmers were offered a total 160 yuan (in the first 3 years) per mu for setting aside sloping land over 25° and planting trees, providing the seedling survival rate passed the standard in annual inspection. Afforestation was divided into ecological forests, subsidized for 8 years, and economic forests, subsidized for 5 years. For example, of the three villages in Zhifanggou catchment, Zhifanggou, Washuta and Siyaoxian, Zhifanggou and Washuta villages were assigned ecological forests and Siyaoxian economic forests. Afforestation Joint effort has been devoted for local implementation of the program, including terracing gentle slopes (less than 25°) financially supported by the local government; providing agricultural extension services by local extension agencies especially on greenhouse crop management, fruit growing, and livestock breeding; fostering off – farm employment market; and offering easier access to loans from the Agricultural Bank of China, especially to those farmers who were engaged in horticultural production.

Considerable changes have taken place for the participant rural households as a result of the program, the most apparent being contraction of the land area. For example, around 53.5% of the farmland in Zhifanggou catchment had been withdrawn from agricultural production as a result of GfG by 2003. The population engaged in agricultural production decreased from 523 to 501, most of which were due to out – migration. The income from non – agricultural activities at the catchment scale increased by 32.5%, while agricultural production decreased by 16.5% in 2003 (provided by Wang Jijun, ISWC, CAS). For Xiannangou catchment, the cultivated land decreased from 5.34 km^2 in 2000 to 3.87 km^2, while forest land (including woodland and shrub – land) and grassland increased from 13.75 km^2 to 18.54 km^2, and 27.09 km^2 to 30.21 km^2, respectively (Dang et al., 2008). In 2000, they observed a major reverse in sloping land cultivation, that sloping cultivated land amounted to only 50% of the total cultivated land area. Till 2005, all of the land was terraced, funded by the government.

Chapter 4   Agricultural TFP and Efficiency Change Induced by GfG

4. 1   Specific Objectives

As has been discussed in Chapter 1, given the large operating scale, huge public investment, and profound environment and well – being implications, the effectiveness and sustainability of the program are of great importance for all the stakeholder involved.

Measured as the ratio of aggregate output to aggregate input, Total Factor Productivity (TFP), has significant environmental and economic implications in context of land retirement. Increases in TFP contribute to total agricultural production that would offset or even outweigh the production loss resulting from the loss of arable land. This not only benefits food security and poverty alleviation and encourages surplus labor to shift to other occupations, but also demotivates farmers to reclaim land later. In this study, we therefore try to study farm TFP change of the participating households, find its sources and determinant factors.

4. 2 Methods

We calculated the TFP change using a Data – Envelopment – Analysis based Malmquist TFP index with distance functions for the farms before and after the first phase of the program. We then decomposed the index into technological growth and technical efficiency change, and further decomposed the latter into pure technical efficiency change and scale efficiency change, to draw inferences about the primary drivers for TFP growth. And then we compare the relative technical efficiency before and after the program. Finally, we used Ordinary Least Square (OLS) regression analysis to investigate the factors affecting TFP growth, technological growth, and technical efficiency change, with a focus on the impact of the measures taken in the program.

4. 2. 1 Malmquist TFP Index

Using the distance functions introduced by Malmquist (1953), Caves et al. (1982) proposed "a framework for input, output, and productivity measurement that does not proceed from a continuous time representation", which they named as Malmquist Index.

Let $x = (x_1, \cdots, x_n) \in R_{N+}$ denote an input vector and $y = (y_1, \cdots, y_n) \in R_{N+}$ an output vector, we can get an production possibility set at time s by:

$$P^s(x) = \{(x, y): x \text{ can produce } y\} \tag{4-1}$$

Assuming constant return to scale (CRS), the output distance func-

◇ 退耕还林政策与黄土高原地区农户可持续生计：基于生产率和效率的实证研究
Grain for Green Program and Sustainable Agriculture and Rural Livelihoods of the Loess
Plateau in China：Empirical Studies with Measurement of Productivity and Efficiency

tion with technology at time s, the initial period, can be defined as：

$$d^s(x, y) = \inf\left\{\theta: \left(x, \frac{y}{\theta}\right) \in P^s(x)\right\} \qquad (4-2)$$

This function completely characterizes the technology at s, in the direction that frontier (or maximum possible) output can be produced given certain amounts of inputs. Here, θ is a scalar, and its value is the efficiency score for each production unit. It satisfies $0 < \theta \leqslant 1$, where a value of 1 indicating a point on the frontier of technology and hence a fully technically efficient production activity.

Similarly, we can define a distance function in relation to technology at time t, the final period, as

$$d^t(x,y) = \inf\left[\theta: \left(x, \frac{y}{\theta}\right) \in P^t(x)\right] \qquad (4-3)$$

Thus, the Malmquist TFP index, which measures the TFP growth between time s and t, can be defined as

$$M^s = \frac{d^s(x^t, y^t)}{d^s(x^s, y^s)} \qquad (4-4)$$

if we take technology at time s as a benchmark, and as

$$M^t = \frac{d^t(x^t, y^t)}{d^t(x^s, y^s)} \qquad (4-5)$$

if we take technology at time t as a benchmark.

To avoid arbitrariness in choosing the benchmark, we follow Färe et al. (1994a) to define the Malmquist TFP index as the geometric mean of the above two indices：

$$M(x^s, y^s, x^t, y^t) = \left[\frac{d^s(x^t, y^t)}{d^s(x^s, y^s)} \times \frac{d^t(x^t, y^t)}{d^t(x^s, y^s)}\right]^{1/2} \qquad (4-6)$$

which is equivalent to：

$$M(x^s, y^s, x^t, y^t) = \frac{d^t(x^t, y^t)}{d^s(x^s, y^s)} \times \left[\frac{d^s(x^t, y^t)}{d^t(x^t, y^t)} \times \frac{d^s(x^s, y^s)}{d^t(x^s, y^s)}\right]^{1/2}$$

$$(4-7)$$

Here, the ratio outside the brackets measures the relative technical efficiency change between time s and t, which can be interpreted as the effect of inefficient farms catching up with better ones (also called catch – up). Farms catch up with the leading farms if they get closer to the frontier; and fall behind if they get further from the frontier. The geometric mean of the two ratios inside the brackets captures the shift in technology between the two periods, or "technological growth" (also called innovation). Expansion of frontier occurs mainly due to technological advances or infrastructure investment. In the case of an upward expansion, we call it "technological progress", and a downward expansion, "technological regress".

Allowing variable return to scale (VRS), Färe et al. (1994b) further decomposed the index into:

$$M(x^s, y^s, x^t, y^t) = \frac{d_V^t(x^t, y^t)}{d_V^s(x^s, y^s)} \left[\frac{d_V^s(x^s, y^s)}{d_V^t(x^t, y^t)} \times \frac{d_C^t(x^t, y^t)}{d_C^s(x^s, y^s)}\right]$$

$$\left[\frac{d_C^s(x^t, y^t)}{d_C^t(x^t, y^t)} \times \frac{d_C^s(x^s, y^s)}{d_C^t(x^s, y^s)}\right]^{1/2} \qquad (4-8)$$

where subscript "V" stands for VRS, "C" for CRS assumption. The first term measures the relative technical efficiency change between time s and t if VRS is assumed; it represents changes in managerial skills "to produce more with less", and is referred to as pure technical efficiency change. The second term measures the change in the ratio of the distance function satisfying CRS to the distance function satisfying VRS, so it represents the efforts of farms to move to the optimum scale and is called scale efficiency

◇ 退耕还林政策与黄土高原地区农户可持续生计：基于生产率和效率的实证研究
Grain for Green Program and Sustainable Agriculture and Rural Livelihoods of the Loess
Plateau in China: Empirical Studies with Measurement of Productivity and Efficiency

change. In another word, technical efficiency (TE) change is the product
of pure technical efficiency (PTE) change and scale efficiency (SE)
change. The third term, as mentioned above, is technological growth. Any
value greater or less than 1 indicates positive or negative growth, respectively, and a value equal to 1 indicates stagnation for the specified efficient or
technology change indicator.

4.2.2 Data Envelopment Analysis

Both Data Envelopment Analysis (DEA), the non-parametric method, and Stochastic Frontier Analysis (SFA), the parametric method can
be used to estimate the distance functions that constitute the Malmquist TFP
index. DEA gained more popularity over SFA recent years. It requires no assumptions about the form of the production function and the distribution of the
underlying data and thus is less sensitive to misspecification and unlike parametric methods, is not subject to assumptions about the distribution of the error
term (see more comparison between parametric and nonparametric method, refer to Bauer et al., 1998). We construct an output-oriented Malmquist TFP
index using the distance functions calculated from a DEA Programming.

Following Färe et al. (1994b), suppose there are K farms (indexed
by k) using N inputs (indexed by n) to produce M products (indexed by
m), x_n^{ks} and y_m^{ks} denote the nth input and mth output for the kth farm at time
s, the base time (x_n^{kt} and y_m^{kt} denote the nth input and mth output for the kth
farm at time t, the current time, accordingly).

The data set is given by $\{(x^{k,i}, y^{k,i}): k = 1, \cdots, K; i = s, t\}$

Assuming CRS technology, technical efficiency relative to the reference
technology at time s(or t), $d_C^s(x^{k's}, y^{k's})$ (or $d_C^t(x^{k't}, y^{k't})$), can be cal-

culated by solving the following linear programming:

$$[d_C^s(x^{k's}, y^{k's})]^{-1} = \max_{z,\theta} \theta^{k's}$$

$$\text{s. t. } \theta^{k's} y_m^{k's} \leqslant \sum_{k=1}^{K} z^{ks} y_m^{ks} \ (m = 1, \cdots, M) \tag{4-9}$$

$$\sum_{k=1}^{K} z^{ks} x_n^{ks} \leqslant x_n^{k's} \ (n = 1, \cdots, N)$$

$$z^{ks} \geqslant 0 \ (k = 1, \cdots, K)$$

In the case that the technology and observations come from different period, e. g. , $d_C^s(x^{k't}, y^{k't})$, technical efficiency can be computed by solving the following linear programming:

$$[d_C^s(x^{k't}, y^{k't})]^{-1} = \max_{z,\theta} \theta^{k't}$$

$$\text{s. t. } \quad \theta^{k't} y_m^{k't} \leqslant \sum_{k=1}^{K} z^{ks} y_m^{ks} \ (m = 1, \cdots, M) \tag{4-10}$$

$$\sum_{k=1}^{K} z^{ks} x_n^{ks} \leqslant x_n^{k't} \ (n = 1, \cdots, N)$$

$$z^{ks} \geqslant 0 (k = 1, \cdots, K)$$

Similarly, we can calculate $d_C^t(x^{k's}, y^{k's})$.

We can calculate distance functions under VRS, $d_V^s(x^{k's}, y^{k's})$ and $d_V^t(x^{k't}, y^{k't})$, by adding the $\sum_{k=1}^{K} z^{ks} = 1$ constraint(Färe et al. , 1994b).

4. 3   Model and Data

4. 3. 1   Inputs and Outputs for Agricultural TFP Change Estimation, Decomposition and the Explanatory Variables

To calculate the Change in TFP after the execution of the program and

◇ 退耕还林政策与黄土高原地区农户可持续生计：基于生产率和效率的实证研究
Grain for Green Program and Sustainable Agriculture and Rural Livelihoods of the Loess
Plateau in China: Empirical Studies with Measurement of Productivity and Efficiency

to identify its sources, we collected data on agricultural outputs and inputs (Table 4 – 1) for 1999, the year before the initiation of the program, and 2007, the last year of the first phase. As shown in Table 4 – 1, we adopt the most common two outputs (*Crop production* and *Livestock production*), and three inputs (*Land*, *Labor* and *Material and capital*) model. Here crops include millet, soybean, maize, potato, fruits, melon and vegetables, while livestock includes cattle, sheep, pigs, chickens, and their products including eggs, milk, and wool. To avoid the effects of currency inflation, we deflated the market value of the data by the GDP deflator (National Bureau of Statistics of China, 2008).

Table 4 – 1　Inputs and Outputs Used to Calculate TFP Growth and Its Sources

	Variable	Definition
Outputs	*Crop production* (thousand yuan)	Market value of crops produced on the farm
	Livestock production (thousand yuan)	Market value of animals and their products produced on the farm
Inputs	*Land* (mu)	Cultivated land on the farm
	Labor (person)	Number of labors in crop and livestock production on the farm, adjusted by actual working hours
	Material and capital (thousand yuan)	Seed, fertilizer, fodder, fuel, pesticide, irrigation, depreciation and maintenance cost of machinery and building, wages, rent

Previous studies have shown that the variation in the individual, household, and institutional environment characteristics partly explains the differences in agricultural TFP growth, technological growth and TE change. We assume the variances of the policy participation are also associated with them. After checking the data for the possible impact of multicollinearity (and this shall apply hereafter in each case study), we chose the following explanatory variables out of our limited database: *Age*, *Health_ status*, *Education*, *Conservation_ payments*, *Off – farm_ income_ increase*, *Credit*, *Land_ terracing*, and *Extension_ services*(Table 4 – 3).

The characteristics of the householders, who are generally the decision – makers or who play a key role in agricultural production and influence family activities, are important factors that affect TFP growth and its sources. Here we include their *Age*, *Health_ status*, and *Education* as the explanatory variables. We should note that *Health_ status* is given as a dummy variable, that we set 1 for those households who had not suffered a chronic or major disease in the past eight years and we set 0 for those who had. We acknowledge that the standard of judgment used here is coarse, owing to the limited data availability. Following Fan et al. (2004), we assign 0, 5, 8, and 12 years for householders who are illiterate or semi – illiterate, primary school diploma, junior high school diploma, and senior high school diploma, respectively.

Variables of *Conservation_ payments*, *Off – farm_ income_ increase*, *Credit*, *Land_ terracing*, and *Extension_ services*, are included to reflect the impact of the specific measures of GfG. Lack of capital limits the purchase of inputs and efficiency – improving equipment and thus discourages the efficient allocation of resources and adoption of technology. We reckon here that, conservation payments, income from off – farm employment, and loans from the banks help the farmers to break out the capital limitations and make optimal decisions on agricultural production. *Conservation_ payments* is estimated as the eight – year(1999 to 2007)average government conservation payment to households. Since the dependent variable is to reflect a trend(or change), we use the change in the proportion of off – farm income to total

◇ 退耕还林政策与黄土高原地区农户可持续生计：基于生产率和效率的实证研究
Grain for Green Program and Sustainable Agriculture and Rural Livelihoods of the Loess
Plateau in China: Empirical Studies with Measurement of Productivity and Efficiency

household income(*Off – farm_ income_ increase*)to reflect the impact of off – farm activities and its income. For the variable of *Credit*, as in our study area, farmers have only limited access to credit for greenhouse building and livestock barn, so we used the ratio of the sum of loans obtained in the past eight years to total household assets as a substitute for that of the current credit. Terracing slopes not only reduces soil erosion but also retains the water, thus is expected to increase crop yield. *Land_ terracing* is given as the percentage of terraced land area to that of the total land areas. The program also involves more intensive extension services to the participating households. *Extension_ services* is given as a dummy variable: 1 if the households received extension services and 0 otherwise.

No abnormal climate was observed in the 2 years, so we ignored the impact of weather. Our priori expectation is that all the variables positively affect agricultural TFP growth and its sources.

4. 3. 2　Descriptive Statistics of the Data

Descriptive statistics of the input and output data are shown in Table 4 – 2, and that of the explanatory data are in Table 4 – 3. Eight years after the introduction of the program, the average area of cultivated land per farm had decreased by 38. 7% as a result of setting – aside sloping land; the labor force had decreased by 16. 3% , most of which had shifted to non – agricultural production(refer to Table 4 – 3 that the proportion of off – farm income has increased by 13. 5%); and material and capital input had increased by 24. 5% on average, most of which resulted from increase in the usage of fertilizer, irrigation facilities, tractor and greenhouses. For the agricultural output, while livestock production had increased by 3. 8% , crop production had increased significantly, by 46. 1% on average.

Table 4 – 2 Descriptive Statistics of Inputs and Outputs to Estimate Agricultural TFP

Year		Outputs		Inputs		
		Crop production	Livestock production	Labor	Land	Material and Capital
1999	Mean	9. 200	2. 763	2. 126	15. 632	1. 622
	SD	8. 762	1. 785	0. 798	13. 234	1. 290
	Min	0. 879	0. 000	0. 700	1. 200	0. 027
	Max	23. 150	6. 500	5. 000	64. 000	5. 957
2007	Mean	13. 441	2. 868	1. 779	9. 580	2. 020
	SD	13. 475	6. 104	0. 488	4. 574	2. 385
	Min	0. 718	0. 000	1. 000	0. 800	0. 022
	Max	69. 960	60. 000	4. 000	23. 500	12. 255

Table 4 – 3 Descriptive Statistics of Explanatory Variables for

Agricultural TFP Change and Its Sources

Variables	Mean	SD	Min	Max
Age(years)	46. 821	9. 587	22. 000	75. 000
Health_ status(0/1)	0. 889	0. 323	0. 000	1. 000
Education(years)	4. 446	3. 683	0. 000	11. 000
Conservation_ payments(thousand yuan)	3. 246	3. 921	0. 640	37. 180
Off – farm_ income_ increase(%)	0. 135	0. 276	– 0. 654	0. 954
Credit(%)	0. 024	0. 104	0. 000	0. 800
Land_ terracing(mu)	1. 195	3. 376	0. 000	14. 000
Extension_ services(0/1)	0. 610	0. 492	0. 000	1. 000

The reason for an increase in crop production with a shrunk cultivated land area is twofold. On one hand, it resulted from the increase in land productivity owing to the soil and water conservation practices, especially terracing slope lands, and the introduction of new seeds and technology like

◇ 退耕还林政策与黄土高原地区农户可持续生计：基于生产率和效率的实证研究
Grain for Green Program and Sustainable Agriculture and Rural Livelihoods of the Loess
Plateau in China: Empirical Studies with Measurement of Productivity and Efficiency

using plastic coversheets to keep soil moisture content and temperature, etc. , on the other hand, resulted from the shift from extensive, subsistence production to intensive, cash production. The share of land under cultivation for cash crops including fruits, melon and vegetables increased from 7% to 26. 4% after the execution of the program(Table 4 – 4).

Table 4 – 4　Land Productivity and Land Share for the Major
Crop Products in 1999 and 2007

Crops	1999			2007		
	Average area of cultivated land(mu)	Land share (%)	Yield (kg/mu)	Average area of cultivated land (mu)	Land share (%)	Yield (kg/mu)
Millet	5. 659	0. 362	95. 465	0. 968	0. 101	137. 238
Soybean	4. 877	0. 312	94. 613	1. 552	0. 162	126. 859
Maize	2. 485	0. 159	279. 953	2. 845	0. 297	426. 564
Potato	1. 548	0. 099	431. 526	1. 159	0. 121	649. 981
Fruits	0. 922	0. 059	1, 008. 957	1. 380	0. 144	1, 225. 683
Melon	0. 078	0. 005	2, 233. 784	0. 795	0. 083	2, 786. 650
Vegetables	0. 063	0. 004	6, 199. 185	0. 881	0. 092	6, 899. 600
Total	15. 632			9. 580		

4. 4　Results and Discussions

4. 4. 1　Agricultural TFP Change, Technological Growth, and TE Change

TFP change and its decomposition were estimated using DEA – Solver

Pro 5. 0(all the other analysis hereafter is performed using the same computer program). Table 4 – 5 shows the TFP growth result for the farms participating in the program. The results suggest that TFP rose by 49. 6% on average. Eighty – four households(75%)showed increased TFP as a result of the program. Technological progress, or the shift in best practice technology, was the only contributor to TFP growth of the farms. In contrast, retrogression of technical efficiency, or slackened catch – up effect, prevented TFP from improving further.

Table 4 –5   Estimated Malmquist Index and the Decomposition Result

	Technological Growth	TE Change	PTE Change	SE Change	TFP Change
	(1)	(2) = (3) × (4)	(3)	(4)	(5) = (1) × (2)
Mean	1. 748	0. 856	0. 879	0. 974	1. 496
SD	0. 682	0. 451	0. 413	0. 254	0. 953
Min	1. 139	0. 135	0. 138	0. 291	0. 328
Max	4. 286	2. 688	2. 595	1. 841	6. 487

The adoption of better technologies led to dramatic improvements in agricultural production, with a range of 1. 139 to 4. 286 and an average of 1. 748. This might be a result of the specified measures in the program, like land terracing, support for green – house farming and fostering of livestock farming, or through financial support, which allowed farms to take advantage of the modern facilities, like tractor, coversheet, greenhouses, irrigation facilities or even improved seeds.

The farmers witnessed a retrogress in technical efficiency of 14. 4% on average. This implies that many of the farmers had not adapted well to the improved technology and had thus failed to catch up with those better – off.

◇ 退耕还林政策与黄土高原地区农户可持续生计：基于生产率和效率的实证研究

Grain for Green Program and Sustainable Agriculture and Rural Livelihoods of the Loess Plateau in China: Empirical Studies with Measurement of Productivity and Efficiency

To trace the sources of the decrease in technical efficiency, we decomposed it into pure technical efficiency and scale efficiency effect, as shown in columns 3 and 4 of Table 4 – 5. The change in scale efficiency had little effect, decreasing by only 2.6% on average. Anyway, the result still suggests that more farmers have failed to operate at an optimum scale after execution of the program. This might be a result of the decreasing cultivated land area. The dominant contributor to the decrease in technical efficiency was pure technical efficiency change, which decreased by 12.1%. This decline can be interpreted as a general retrogression in the ability of the farmers to manage agricultural production under the new technology. That is, even though the farmers used conventional technology in 1999 efficiently, they are not as successfully managing the agricultural production as their leading farms under the new technology.

4.4.2 Technical Efficiency in 1999 and 2007

We should keep in mind that DEA generates relative efficiency measurements that make no sense if compared between different periods directly, as the relative efficiency are based on different technology levels. We plotted the frequency distribution of technical efficiencies for the sample farms in 1998 and 2007, under the CRS assumption, to see the changes in the distribution of the efficiencies (Figure 4 – 1).

The average efficiency in 1999 was 0.712 with a standard deviation of 0.201, whereas that in 2007 was 0.609 with a stand deviation of 0.286. Figure 4 – 1 indicates that the farmers had a more even efficiency distribution after the execution of the program. Both distributions show bimodal features. One mode is around 0.5 – 0.6 and another higher mode is around

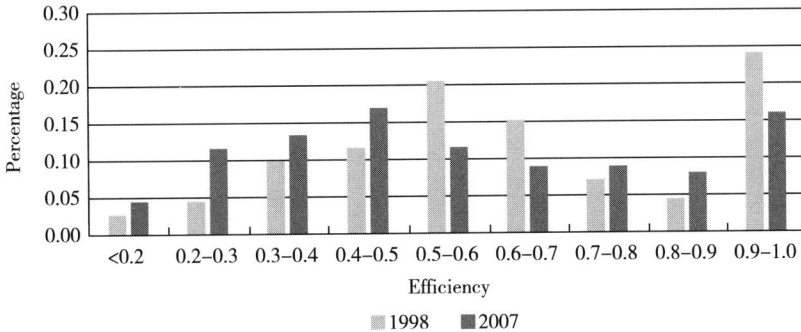

Figure 4 – 1　Frequency Distribution of CRS TE of the Farms in 1999 and 2007

0. 9 – 1. 0 in 1999; while in 2007, one mode is around 0. 4 – 0. 5 and another lower mode is around 0. 9 – 1. 0. This suggests that there were more
farms close to or had reached the best practice frontier in 1999. This result
accords with our previous finding that only a few farms caught – up with the
leading farms after the execution of the program.

We were also interested in the change in farms' efficiency rankings after the execution of the program to see whether the program benefited the
originally inefficient farms. To test the relationship between the efficiency
ranks before and after the program, we used Spearman's Rank Correlation
Analysis. The correlation value in this method ranges from – 1. 0 (perfect
negative correlation), through 0(no correlation), to + 1. 0(perfect positive
correlation). To avoid the same ranks resulting from the same technical efficiency values, technical efficiency was given as super – efficiency value,
which is measured relative to a frontier derived without the farm under consideration.

The rank correlation between 1999 and 2007 is statistically significant
and positive but not high, with a value of only 0. 312, which reflects low

◇ 退耕还林政策与黄土高原地区农户可持续生计：基于生产率和效率的实证研究

Grain for Green Program and Sustainable Agriculture and Rural Livelihoods of the Loess Plateau in China: Empirical Studies with Measurement of Productivity and Efficiency

ranking stability for the farms (Table 4 – 6). Among the eleven efficient farms in 1999, only two of them remained efficient in 2007; and that for the formerly inefficient farms, seventeen improved greatly, six of which even leaped to the top. This result suggests that all the measures in the program taken together, it preferentially emphasized farms with an unfavorable initial state.

Table 4 – 6   Spearman's Rank Correlation Coefficient

	Super – efficiency scores in 1999	
	coefficient	Two – tailed P value
Super – efficiency scores in 2007	0. 312	0. 041

4. 4. 3   Determinants of TFP Change, Technological Growth, and TE Change

The OLS estimates of the effect of the explanatory variables on TFP change, technological growth, and technical efficiency change are revealed in Table 4 – 7. The result shows that *Land_ terracing* is the only variable that is significantly related to all of the three indices. The coefficients are positive, which suggests that land terracing benefited TFP growth, technological growth as well as technical efficiency change. The positive relationship with TFP growth and technical efficiency change, as we supposed, might result from improved water and nutrient holding capacity under leveled land. And the positive relationship of land terracing and technological growth might be related to the fact that it makes possible of the farmers to employ facilities like tractors.

Table 4 – 7　Factors Explaining TFP Change, Technological Growth and TE Change

Independent Variables	Dependent Variables		
	TFP Change	Technological Growth	TE Change
Constant	1. 253 ***	1. 190 ***	1. 474 ***
Age	– 0. 028	– 0. 001	– 0. 012 **
Health_ status	0. 250	0. 317	0. 011
Education	0. 010	0. 049 **	– 0. 017
Conservation_ payments	0. 077	0. 196 **	– 0. 043
Off –farm_ income_ increase	– 1. 208 **	– 1. 084 **	– 0. 030
Credit	3. 835 **	1. 992 **	0. 728
Land_ terracing	0. 139 ***	0. 081 ***	0. 032 **
Extension_ services	0. 274	0. 780 ***	0. 022

Note: The symbols *, **, *** indicate statistical significance at the 1%, 5%, and 10% levels, respectively.

For the variables we had reckoned to help break the capital limitations, we find out that there is positive relationship between *Credit* and TFP growth and technological growth, and positive relationship between *Conservation_ payments* and technological growth. However, the increase in the proportion of off – farm income is negatively related to technological growth and TFP change. According to previous studies (e. g. , Nehring and Fernandez – Cornejo, 2005), off – farm employment of the surplus labors would not only raise total household income, improving the potential to invest in capital – intensive efficiency – improving practices, but also broaden the farmers' horizon, facilitating imitation and competition, therefore improve their efficiency, technology, and TFP. The negative relationship, however, might imply that competent labor forces, or even capital, are distracted to more profitable non – agricultural activities. In other words, off – farm activities compete with farm activities (Pfeiffer et al. , 2009; Solís et al. , 2009). In

◇ 退耕还林政策与黄土高原地区农户可持续生计：基于生产率和效率的实证研究
Grain for Green Program and Sustainable Agriculture and Rural Livelihoods of the Loess
Plateau in China： Empirical Studies with Measurement of Productivity and Efficiency

contrast, the impact of *Credit* is noteworthy. And the result is consistent to the fact that loan from the bank generally goes to farms engaged in greenhouse vegetable production for cover – sheeting; and pig or cattle breeding farms for purchasing feed additives and other innovations.

The result shows that, contacting the farmers with training and extension services(*Extension_ services*)improves farmers' technological level significantly as expected. The interpretation in our study is that, introducing new seeds and varieties, spreading of the irrigation, temperature, pest control and other vegetable and fruits management practices, and breeding and feeding practices by the local public agencies through GfG, have significantly improved the technology level for the sample farms.

The coefficient of the age of householders on technical efficiency change is significant and negative, which is consistent to Tauer and Nazibrola (2000)'s work. The implication is that the older farmers were less successfully receptive or adapting to the new technology and practices.

4.5　Conclusions

Our results show that the program had greatly improved TFP for farm households in the Zhifanggou catchment, solely through technological progress. In contrast, technical efficiency decreased as a result of decreases in both pure technical efficiency and scale efficiency. Thus, even though the program had improved the technology available to the farmers, the farmers' ability to produce more agricultural products under improved technology had decreased. Only a few farms successfully managed to catch up with the leading farms after the execution of the program, although the distribution of technical efficiency has become more equitable. Farms with a poorer technical efficiency benefited more than the better performers.

Land terracing and access to credit contributed significantly to TFP growth and technological growth. Land terracing also contributed significantly to technical efficiency change. Extension services contributed significantly to technological growth. And age of the householder withdraws technical efficiency change significantly. It is noteworthy that the impact of conservation subsidy is not as effective as expected, and off – farm activities might even compete with farm activities for resources. Thus, we hereby suggest that policy – makers focus resources on terracing sloping lands, improving access to credit, and offering extension services during next phase of GfG.

Chapter 5   Farm Efficiency and Its Determinant Factors

5. 1   Specific Objectives

Agricultural production can be improved by intensifying agricultural inputs, adopting new technology, or improving efficiency (the latter two combined into TFP). However, options to expand agricultural production by intensifying inputs within the context of GfG are limited because the program not only directly decreases the cultivated land area, but also encourages off – farm employment. And the result from previous study suggests that as a result of several years' efforts by the program, even though the technology available to farmers has greatly improved, farm efficiency under the improved technology has not. Therefore, the most effective way for farms to increase their agricultural production is to improve production efficiency. The objective of this study, is therefore to find out the efficiencies for farms under the prevailing circumstances, including the improved technology, the shrunk cultivated land area and others, and find out the determinant factors for the efficiencies.

5. 2   Methods

We used a two – stage approach to fulfill the obligations. First, we used DEA to estimate efficiencies, including cost efficiency, technical efficiency, pure technical efficiency, allocative efficiency and scale efficiency, excluding discretionary variables. Second, we used farm – specific socio – economic variables and the variables to reflect the involvement of farm households in the specific measures of the program, in an OLS regression framework to explain variation in measured efficiencies.

5. 2. 1   Estimation of Efficiencies: PTE, TE, CE, SE and AE

5. 2. 1. 1   Technical and Pure Technical Efficiency

Following Färe et al. (1994c), suppose that K farms (indexed by k) use N inputs (indexed by n) to produce M products (indexed by m), we can estimate the input – oriented technical efficiency of the ith farm, under the assumption of CRS, $TE_i(y_i, x_i)$, by solving the following linear programme:

$$TE_i(y_i, x_i) = \min_{\theta_i, \lambda} \theta_i$$

subject to

$$-y_{im} + \sum_{k=1}^{K} y_{km}\lambda_k \geqslant 0 \quad (m = 1, 2, \cdots, M) \tag{5-1}$$

$$\theta_i x_{in} - \sum_{k=1}^{K} x_{kn}\lambda_k \geqslant 0 \quad (n = 1, 2, \cdots, N)$$

$$\lambda_k \geqslant 0 \quad (k = 1, 2, \cdots, K)$$

◇ 退耕还林政策与黄土高原地区农户可持续生计：基于生产率和效率的实证研究
Grain for Green Program and Sustainable Agriculture and Rural Livelihoods of the Loess
Plateau in China: Empirical Studies with Measurement of Productivity and Efficiency

where x_i and y_i are the input and output vectors of the ith farm, respectively; x_{kn} and y_{km} are the nth input and mth output of the kth farm; λ_k represents the weights to be used in the inputs for the kth farm to achieve efficiency; and θ_i is the technical efficiency of the ith farm, bound by 0 and 1, where 1 indicates efficient and less than 1 indicates inefficient.

The technical efficiency under VRS, pure technical efficiency, PTE_i (y_i, x_i), can be derived by adding the convexity constraint $\sum_{k=1}^{K} \lambda_k = 1$, which benchmarks the farm against farms of a similar size.

5. 2. 1. 2　Cost and Allocative Efficiency

To estimate the allocative efficiency of the ith farm, we first need to calculate cost efficiency by solving the following cost – minimizing DEA model under the assumption of CRS:

$$MC_i(y_i, x'_{in}, c_{in}) = \min_{x'_{in}, \lambda_i} (c_{in} \times x'_{in})$$

subject to

$$- y_{im} + \sum_{k=1}^{K} y_{km}\lambda_k \geq 0 \quad (m = 1, 2, \cdots, M) \quad\quad (5-2)$$

$$x'_{in} - \sum_{k=1}^{K} x_{kn}\lambda_k \geq 0 \quad (n = 1, 2, \cdots, N)$$

$$\lambda_k \geq 0 \quad (k = 1, 2, \cdots, K)$$

$$\sum_{k=1}^{K} \lambda_k = 1$$

where MC_i (y_i, x'_{in}, c_{in}) is the minimum total cost for the ith farm under CRS; c_{in} is the price of the nth input used by the ith farm for agricultural production; and x'_{in} is the combination cost – minimizing nth input used by the ith farm. As the actual cost for the ith farm is given by $c_{in} \times x_{in}$, cost efficiency, the ratio of minimum to actual cost, is expressed by

$$CE_i(y_i,\ x_{in},\ c_{in}) = [MC_i(y_i,\ x'_{in},\ c_{in})]/(c_{in} \times x_{in}) \qquad (5-3)$$

The ith farm is cost efficient when $CE_i = 1$.

Allocative efficiency is then computed by:

$$AE_i(y_i,\ x_{in},\ c_{in}) = [CE_i(y_i,\ x_{in},\ c_{in})]/TE_i(y_i,\ x_i) \qquad (5-4)$$

under the assumption of CRS (Farrell, 1957).

5. 2. 1. 3　Scale Efficiency

The scale efficiency of the ith farm is obtained by dividing technical efficiency by pure technical efficiency:

$$SE_i(y_i,\ x_i) = \frac{TE_i(y_i,\ x_i)}{PTE_i(y_i,\ x_i)} \qquad (5-5)$$

where $SE = 1$ represents scale efficient (under both CRS and VRS) and $0 \leqslant SE < 1$ represents scale inefficient, which can be either increasing returns – to – scale (IRS) or decreasing returns – to – scale (DRS).

Following Coelli et al. (2005), the property of returns – to – scale (RTS) in operation can be detected by replacing the convexity constraint $\sum_{k=1}^{K} \lambda_k = 1$ (VRS) with $\sum_{k=1}^{K} \lambda_k \leqslant 1$ (the assumption of non – increasing returns – to – scale, NIRS) when estimating technical efficiency and then comparing the NIRS and VRS efficiency scores. If the two scores are equal, the farm is operating at decreasing returns – to – scale; and if not, at increasing returns – to – scale. Finally, if technical efficiency under CRS equals that under VRS, then it is operating under CRS by definition. In the case NIRSTE, CRSTE and VRSTE are all equal to 1, it is the most productive scale size (MPSS).

5. 2. 2　Second – stage Regression Analysis

In efficiency analysis, the second – stage regression usually involves a

◆ 退耕还林政策与黄土高原地区农户可持续生计：基于生产率和效率的实证研究

Grain for Green Program and Sustainable Agriculture and Rural Livelihoods of the Loess Plateau in China: Empirical Studies with Measurement of Productivity and Efficiency

Tobit model（because the efficiency scores are censored between 0 and 1； e. g. , Chavas et al. , 2005； Fletschner, 2008）. However recently there comes the debate of the appropriateness of Tobit model in the second stage, especially since the work of Simar and Wilson （2007）. They argued that efficiency scores generated from DEA method are serially correlated and proposed a seven – step double bootstrapping procedure to produce consistent estimates in the second stage. Banker and Natarajan （2008）, on the other side, demonstrated that a two – stage approach comprising a DEA model followed by an OLS （or MLE） model yields consistent estimators when data are generated by a monotone increasing and concave production function （as is the presumed by most production functions） separable from a parametric function of the contextual variables. Other researchers deem DEA "scores" as simply a statistical or theoretical measure of distance to an observed "best practice frontier" （e. g. , Hoff, 2007； McDonald, 2009）, which should not be deemed censored but fractional, and advocate OLS instead of censor regression model like Tobit for a consistent estimator. Given both have sizable followers and the highly computational complexity of Simar and Wilson （2000） approach, we opt for OLS in our efficiency regression model, to provide a consistent and easier way of parameter estimation.

The regression equation takes the following form: $EFF_i = \alpha_0 + \sum_{j=1}^{J} \alpha_{ij} V_{ij} + e_i$, where EFF_i is the efficiency score of the ith farm derived from the first stage estimation； α_0 is the intercept, V_{ij} is the jth of J explanatory variables for the ith farm； and e_i is the error term.

5. 3   Model and Data

5. 3. 1   Inputs and Outputs for Farm Efficiencies Estimation and the Explanatory Variables

To estimate the input – oriented frontier, and thus the efficiency scores for the farms, the quantities and prices of all inputs and the total volumes of outputs were needed. The input variables, for which data were collected at the farm level, included *Land*; *Labors*; *Seed*; *Fertilizer*; *Fuel*; *Young animals*; *Fodder*. Except for land and labor, the quantities of all inputs were estimated by dividing total expenditures by the average of sampled prices. The prices for land and labor in 2007 are taken from the Shaanxi Statistic Bureau (http: //www. sei. gov. cn/) . The price of labor was given as the average annual net agricultural income at a provincial level, instead of shadow wage – rate, due to data availability. The output variables were *Crop* and *Livestock* (refer to Table 5 – 1) . *Land*, *Labors*, *Crop* and *Livestock* were defined the same as in previous study.

Many studies have investigated the impact of exogenous variables that might influence farm efficiencies (e. g. , Alvarez and Arias, 2004; Karagiannis and Sarris, 2005; Amaza and Ogundari, 2008; Feng, 2008; Latruffe et al. , 2008; Chen et al. , 2009; Tan et al. , 2010) . Bravo – Ureta and Pinheiro (1993) had given a detailed review of the socio – economic variables relevant to farm efficiencies in the developing countries, which provide useful reference for this study. In our model, we have chosen the following variables with better data availability in 2007：*Education*, *Child*, *Land/labor*, *Simpson_ index*, *Conservation_ payments*, *Remittance*, *Tenancy*, *Credit* and *extension_ services* （Table 5 – 2） （we should note that different models have been applied and there is little difference among the models with regard to the important parameters；we only show this model to save space）. The variable of *Education*, *Conservation_ payments*, *Credit* and *extension_ services* is given the same way as in previous study.

Some researcher has recognized the importance of family composition on the livelihoods of rural households, and claimed that the presence of children in a family spares the time of their parent or adult guardian's and affect their decision on farm and off – farm labor supply （e. g., Liang et al., 2012）. And this would affect their efficiency of farm production. We therefore included the variable of *Child*, which is given as a dummy variable, 1 for those family having one or more children under 15 years old, and 0 otherwise. *Land/labor* is also included to take the impact of the land resource endowment into account. This variable is measured as the total land area in mu （15 mu =1 hectare） owned by the households divided by number of adults in the household. Land fragmentation was measured by the *Simpson_ index* in our study, which is defined as $1 - \left(\sum_{s=1}^{S} a_s^2/A_s^2 \right)$; where a_s is the area of the *s*th plot and *A* is the farm's total land area, composed of *S* plots, $\sum_{s=1}^{S} a_s$. We define a plot as a discrete parcel of land physically separated from other land owned by the same household. This index has a value between 0 and 1. A value of 0 means that the farm household has only one parcel or plot of land, which indicates complete land consolidation, whereas a value close to 1 means the household has numerous plots and the farm is "very fragmented". *Remittance* was included to indicate the impact of remittance on farm technical efficiency. *Tenancy* is the rented cultivated land area divided by the total cultivated land area.

5.3.2 Descriptive Statistics of the Data

Descriptive statistics of the data used in this study are shown in Table 5 − 1 and Table 5 − 2.

Table 5 − 1 Descriptive Statistics of Input and Outputs to Estimate Efficiency Scores

			Mean	SD	Min	Max
Outputs		Crop (thousand yuan)	13.441	13.475	0.718	69.960
		Livestock (thousand yuan)	2.868	6.104	0.000	60.000
Inputs	Q	Land (mu)	9.580	4.574	0.800	23.500
		Labor (persons)	1.779	0.488	1.000	4.000
		Seed (kg)	11.172	7.551	0.910	38.960
		Fertilizer (kg)	465.329	428.620	24.000	1,838.000
		Fuel (kg)	0.871	1.874	0.000	11.400
		Young animal (kg)	58.552	107.632	0.000	640.000
		Fodder (kg)	638.259	1,486.056	0.000	15,000.000
	P	Land (thousand yuan/mu)	0.048			
		Labor (thousand yuan/person × year)	2.645			
		Seed (thousand yuan/kg)	0.010			
		Fertilizer (thousand yuan/kg)	0.025			
		Fuel (thousand yuan/kg)	0.006			
		Young animal (thousand yuan/kg)	0.005			
		Fodder (thousand yuan/kg)	0.007			

Note: Here Q refers to quantity and P refers to price; and note that we assume farms faced same input prices.

◇ 退耕还林政策与黄土高原地区农户可持续生计：基于生产率和效率的实证研究
Grain for Green Program and Sustainable Agriculture and Rural Livelihoods of the Loess
Plateau in China: Empirical Studies with Measurement of Productivity and Efficiency

According to Table 5 – 1, the farms are dominated by crop production, and livestock is basically a sideline product, with average income from crop production of 13. 441 thousand yuan and that from livestock production of 2. 868 thousand yuan. Arable land per household is only 9. 580 mu with substantial variability.

We can judge from Table 5 – 2 that the householders in our sample were generally with low education level, almost 1 out of 3 of them have the burden to looking after the children. There is severe fragmentation of the cultivated land resources. Conservation payments accounts for quite a share in household income. And although off – farm income has steadily become an important income source for the households, the remittance is quite limited. Land use right transfer emerged, and rented land amounted to 9. 9% of total cultivated land on average. Access to credit was rather limited. But the agricultural advisory service provided by the local agencies is quite frequent. The statistics are marked by huge variation in the remittance, conservation payments and the proportion of rented land.

Table 5 – 2　Descriptive Statistics of Explanatory Variables for Farm Efficiencies

Variables	Mean	SD	Min	Max
Education (years)	4. 446	3. 683	0. 000	11. 000
Child (0/1)	0. 329	0. 431	0. 000	1. 000
Land/labor (mu/person)	4. 108	3. 140	0. 500	15. 000
Simpson_ index	0. 658	0. 165	0. 000	0. 885
Conservation_ payments (thousand yuan)	3. 246	3. 921	0. 640	37. 180
Remittance (thousand yuan)	0. 239	0. 845	0. 000	2. 000
Tenancy (%)	0. 099	0. 205	0. 000	1. 000
Credit (%)	0. 024	0. 104	0. 000	0. 800
Extension_ services (0/1)	0. 610	0. 492	0. 000	1. 000

5. 4   Results and Discussions

5. 4. 1   Farm Efficiencies

The statistics of the efficiency scores are presented in Table 5 – 3. The results indicate considerable inefficiency in agricultural production.

Table 5 – 3   Statistics of Efficiency Scores

	TE	AE	CE	PTE	SE
Mean	0. 689	0. 389	0. 274	0. 821	0. 819
SD	0. 266	0. 172	0. 183	0. 178	0. 220
Min	0. 105	0. 076	0. 029	0. 344	0. 210
Max	1. 000	1. 000	1. 000	1. 000	1. 000

As cost inefficiency is a result of both allocative inefficiency and technical inefficiency, we can conclude that cost inefficiency (0. 726) is mainly due to allocative inefficiency (0. 611) rather than technical inefficiency (0. 311) . The farmers could reduce costs by 61. 1% choosing more cost – efficient input combinations without compromising output. Technical inefficiency (0. 311) results from both pure technical inefficiency (0. 179) and scale inefficiency (0. 181) . This implies that if all farms were an optimal size, the cost would be decreased by 18. 1% to produce the same output.

Table 5 – 4 shows the distribution of the efficiency scores. More than

◇ 退耕还林政策与黄土高原地区农户可持续生计：基于生产率和效率的实证研究
Grain for Green Program and Sustainable Agriculture and Rural Livelihoods of the Loess
Plateau in China: Empirical Studies with Measurement of Productivity and Efficiency

90% of the cost efficiency and allocative efficiency scores were less than 0.6, whereas nearly 60% of the technical efficiency scores were above 0.6, and 25% were absolutely technical efficient. This is consistent with the result above that farmers were unable to allocate inputs so as to minimize costs, rather than unable to use resources with the greatest technical efficiency. Thirty farms (26.8%) had reached optimal scale but 82 (73.2%) operated with non – optimal scale.

Table 5 – 4   Frequency Distribution of Efficiency Scores

Range	TE	AE	CE	PTE	SE
(0.0 – 0.1]	0	4	17	0	0
(0.1 – 0.2]	3	13	29	0	0
(0.2 – 0.3]	9	15	24	0	3
(0.3 – 0.4]	9	22	20	1	4
(0.4 – 0.5]	6	32	11	3	6
(0.5 – 0.6]	18	18	7	11	9
(0.6 – 0.7]	8	4	1	20	7
(0.7 – 0.8]	16	2	1	17	10
(0.8 – 0.9]	8	0	0	11	14
(0.9 – 1.0)	7	0	0	5	29
1.0	28	2	2	44	30

Statistics related to the returns – to – scale characteristics are given in Table 5 – 5 to explore the details of scale inefficiency. Of the 82 scale inefficient farms, most (69.6%) operated at increasing returns – to – scale (sub – optimal scale), implying that most farms are too small. Farms operating at decreasing returns – to – scale (supra – optimal scale) and constant returns – to – scale (optimal scale) have higher average values of agricultural output than those at sub – optimal scale, and achieved, on average, higher efficiency scores than those operating at sub − optimal scale, suggesting that expanding the size of the farms would improve production efficiencies.

Table 5 − 5　Returns to Scale of Sample Farms

RTS	No. of farms	Average Value					
		Agricultural output (thousand yuan)	TE	AE	CE	PTE	SE
IRS	78	11. 687	0. 570	0. 374	0. 215	0. 758	0. 742
CRS	30	26. 790	0. 985	0. 421	0. 417	0. 985	1. 000
DRS	4	27. 848	0. 797	0. 451	0. 358	0. 819	0. 974

5. 4. 2　Determinants of Farm Efficiencies

Because technical, allocative, and scale efficiency have greater practical implications, we used OLS regression to simulate the relationship between the explanatory variables and the technical, allocative, and scale efficiency scores obtained in the previous section. The results are presented in Table 5 − 6.

Table 5 − 6　Factors Affecting Technical, Allocative and Scale Efficiency

Variable	TE	AE	SE
Constant	0. 972 ***	0. 193 **	0. 873 ***
Education	− 0. 008	0. 004	− 0. 009
Child	− 0. 025	− 0. 014	0. 007
Land/labor	0. 007	0. 001	0. 007 *
Simpson_ index	− 0. 414 ***	0. 125	− 0. 075
Conservation_ payments	0. 008	0. 005	0. 003
Remittance	0. 110 **	0. 015	0. 056 *

◆ 退耕还林政策与黄土高原地区农户可持续生计：基于生产率和效率的实证研究
Grain for Green Program and Sustainable Agriculture and Rural Livelihoods of the Loess
Plateau in China: Empirical Studies with Measurement of Productivity and Efficiency

续表

Variable	TE	AE	SE
Tenancy	− 0. 679	0. 215 **	0. 016 *
Credit	0. 325 *	0. 032	0. 260 *
Extension_ services	0. 173 ***	0. 108 ***	0. 178 ***

Note: The symbols *, **, *** indicate statistical significance at the 1%, 5%, and 10% levels, respectively.

Extension_ services is significantly and positively related to all the three indices. In the previous study, we have found that agricultural TFP has greatly improved, and the major source is the technology improvement. We found in section 5. 4. 1 that agricultural production under improved technology encounters substantial inefficiencies. The inefficiency in agricultural production in developing countries might due to farmers' high degree of unfamiliarity with new technology coupled with poor extension, education, credit and input supply system among others (Alene and Zeller, 2005). Since the introduction of new technologies requires intensive management and information, farmers in developing countries with low literacy rates, poor extension services and inadequate physical infrastructures have great difficulty in adopting new technologies, let alone exploiting their full potentials (Alene and Hassan, 2006). The positive relationship between *Extension_ services* and the efficiency scores suggest that, providing agricultural technical advisory to the farmers provides an extremely effective way of introducing new technologies, and improving the efficiencies of farmer's agricultural production.

There are many studies on the relationship between land rental market participation and farm efficiency in the developing countries. The literature has emphasized the importance of a possible investment disincentive effect derived from insecure land tenure. For example, Latruffe et al. (2008) found rented land is negatively related to farm efficiency and stated that rented – in plots are subject to tenure insecurity, and this may discourage the farmers' utilization of better resource management practices and reduce the farm efficiency. Relatively less attention has been devoted to the allocative impact of land tenure arrangements (Deininger and Jin, 2004) . The transference of land in the rural land rental market generally involves the redistribution of land from less to more efficient producers, therefore increases the allocative efficiency. In our study, *Tenancy* was found to be significantly and positively related to allocative and scale efficiency, and its impact on technical efficiency is insignificant. This might due to the fact that, the farmland tenure system in our study area is characterized by insecure land right, resulted from both the separation of land property right and use right (the former being possessed by the village collective and the latter by the individual farm households) and the occasional administrative reallocations of land by the village collective to adapt to demographic changes (Feng, 2008) . In this case, the farmers who had rented in plots have little or no incentive to invest on them to improve the technical efficiency. However, renting in land resources improves their allocative and scale efficiency indeed.

The positive relationship between *Credit* and technical and scale efficiency, implies that access to credit is likely to enhance the agricultural technical efficiency of the farmers in the study area through the alleviation of capital constraints and thus enables farmers to make timely purchases of inputs that they cannot afford from their own resources. In the study area, credit is generally used for purchase of tractor, construction of greenhouse

◇ 退耕还林政策与黄土高原地区农户可持续生计：基于生产率和效率的实证研究
Grain for Green Program and Sustainable Agriculture and Rural Livelihoods of the Loess
Plateau in China: Empirical Studies with Measurement of Productivity and Efficiency

and livestock shed. In other words, credit facilitates the utilization of the best technology available, and helps to optimize and expand the production scale (as indicated in section 5.4.1, most of the farmers are characterized by increasing returns to scale, therefore expanding their scale of production would improve their production efficiency). Our result is in agreement with Binam et al. (2004), who found a positive impact of credit on technical efficiency.

The *Simpson Index* was negatively related to technical efficiency, in other words, land fragmentation is significantly detrimental to farm technical efficiency. This result is consistent with other studies in China (e.g., Feng, 2008; Chen et al., 2009; Tan et al., 2010). The underlying reason might be that land fragmentation discourages agricultural mechanism, prevents investment in soil conservation and more profitable crops, causes wastage at plot boundaries, increases time spent commuting between plots, and increases loss of industrial inputs such as fertilizers, pesticides and seeds during transport from one plot to another (Burton, 1988; Chen et al., 2009; Rahman and Rahman, 2008; Tan et al., 2010).

It is noteworthy that neither *Conservation_ payments* nor *Off – farm_ work* (to save space, the result of the model including this variable is not put here) is significantly related to the farm efficiencies, but *Remittance* is positively related to technical and scale efficiency. The results suggest that remittances from out – migrant family members might provide a source to help relax the farm's capital constraints to permit investment in efficiency enhancing equipment and technology, and in expanding farm size, but off – farm work alone does not. There are still quite significant institutional constraints for the rural workers to improve their economic status due to the different household registration system (so called " hukou" in Chinese) between rural and urban residents and thus different social welfares.

We had assumed that the presence of children in a family would spare the time and effort of their guardian's, and thus decrease their efficiency of farm production. This study, however, is insignificant. Part of the reason might be the failure to separate the time spent on farming with that on housework and child – care.

5. 5   Conclusions

Our results indicate the existence of substantial inefficiency in agricultural production for the sample farms participating in GfG on the Loess Plateau, suggesting the existence of immense potentials for enhancing production through improvements in efficiency with available technology and resources. The inefficiencies, was partly be explained by insufficient farm size, lack of extension services, lack of access to capital, insecure land tenure and land fragmentation. Providing agricultural technical advisory to the farmers provides an extremely effective way with respect to technical skill introduction and farm management capacity improvement of the farmers. Access of credit for the farmers facilitates the utilization of the best technology available, and helps to optimize their production scale. The current farmland tenure system is characterized by insecure land right, resulted from both the separation of land property right and use right and the occasional administrative reallocations of land by the village collective to adapt to demographic changes (Feng, 2008) . Against such background, even though the land

◇ 退耕还林政策与黄土高原地区农户可持续生计：基于生产率和效率的实证研究
Grain for Green Program and Sustainable Agriculture and Rural Livelihoods of the Loess
Plateau in China：Empirical Studies with Measurement of Productivity and Efficiency

rental market on the Loess Plateau after the program showed to benefit alloca-tive and scale efficiency, it discourages land investment and undermines farm technical efficiency in agricultural production. Alleviating land fragmentation is also significant for improving farm technical efficiency.

We therefore recommend that effort should be made to expand the farm size, even though practical mechanisms by which to achieve this may be difficult to identify. At the very least, it is clear that any further withdrawal of cultivated land from production must be performed in a manner that avoids the deterioration of productive efficiencies, and thus agricultural production, on the remaining land. And even though the result of the regression analysis might be subjected to possible endogeneity between the variables, we still remind policies should be oriented to strengthen the extension and advisory services to the farmers, facilitate their access to credit, provide more secure land tenure, and increase land consolidation.

Chapter 6   Determinant of Off – farm Employment and Household Welfare

6. 1   Specific Objectives

The objective of GfG is to induce sustainable agriculture and rural livelihoods so that the agricultural production improves and surplus labor forces shift to off – farm jobs. In this way, the goal of sustainable development in the less – favored areas is achieved. As reviewed in section 1. 4, however, whether the program, with conservation payment as the principal measure, induced increased off – farm employment and improved household welfare is yet unclear. And due to the intricate relationship between off – farm and farm activities, nor has the impact of off – farm employment on household welfare under the auspices of GfG come to an agreement. There are some signs that off – farm employment might be detrimental to agricultural production according to the result of our previous studies. Thus, the present study aims to contribute to the literature and examine the factors that influence household decisions to participate in off – farm work and estimate the impact of participation on household welfare under the auspices of GfG. We account for the un-

◇ 退耕还林政策与黄土高原地区农户可持续生计：基于生产率和效率的实证研究
Grain for Green Program and Sustainable Agriculture and Rural Livelihoods of the Loess
Plateau in China: Empirical Studies with Measurement of Productivity and Efficiency

observed endogeneity of the off – farm participation decision that may confound its impacts on household welfare employing Endogenous Switching Regression (ESR) method. The treatment and heterogeneity effects of off – farm participation on household welfare are also estimated explicitly within the ESR framework.

6. 2　Methods

6. 2. 1　Analytical Framework

Following the conventional household choice framework, the decision of a farmer to work off the farm is based on a comparison of the market wage of off – farm work and the reservation wage from on – farm work (Singh et al., 1986). Here the reservation wage refers to the minimum wage at which an individual will consent to work. For engagement in off – farm work, it equals the marginal value of a person's time when it is all apportioned to farm and leisure (Owusu et al., 2011). A rational farmer will decide to work off – farm if the potential market wage of off – farm work is higher than the reservation wage from on – farm work and leisure. However, these wage differentials are not observable. What is observed is the decision to participate ($L_i = 1$), or not to participate in off – farm work ($L_i = 0$). According to Huffman and Lange (1989), the probit model describing the off – farm work choices of the household members can be specified as the difference between the utility that a farm household gains from participating or not participating in off – farm work:

$$L_i^* = \alpha Z_i + \mu_i$$

$$L_i = 1, \quad \text{if } L_i^* > 0 \qquad\qquad\qquad (6-1)$$

$$L_i = 0, \quad \text{if } L_i^* \leqslant 0$$

where L_i^* is an unobservable latent variable indicating the probability of a farm household works off the farm; it equals 1 if there are family members participating in off – farm work, and 0 if not; Z_i refers to variables that affect off – farm participation, including conservation payments from the program, farm or household characteristics, formal or informal institutions, etc. ; and μ_i is an error term.

To estimate the relationship between household welfare, Y_i (such as household income and income per capita), and off – farm employment participation, L_i, we start with a linear function:

$$Y_i = \beta X_i + \gamma L_i + \varepsilon_i \qquad\qquad\qquad (6-2)$$

where L_i is the binary variable representing farmer's participation in off – farm work, X_i is a set of variables affecting household welfare, including conservation payments from the program, farm, household or institutional variables, and ε_i is an error term.

However, the decision of household members to participate in off – farm work is likely to be nonrandom and may be dependent on the welfare outcome from participation. In addition, some unobserved characteristics (such as motivation, ability or social networks) might also affect both off – farm participation and its welfare outcome (Owusu et al. , 2011) . In such cases, problems of selection bias and endogeneity may arise and should be corrected to assess the impact of off – farm participation on household welfare. Failure to account for these problems and the use of standard regression techniques would lead to biased results.

◇ 退耕还林政策与黄土高原地区农户可持续生计：基于生产率和效率的实证研究
Grain for Green Program and Sustainable Agriculture and Rural Livelihoods of the Loess
Plateau in China： Empirical Studies with Measurement of Productivity and Efficiency

6. 2. 2 Estimation Strategy

We address the selection bias and endogeneity problems by utilizing the
ESR method （Lokshin and Sajaia, 2004）, because the presence of unobservable factors makes propensity score matching （PSM, which matches observable characteristics） less credible, and the use of cross – sectional survey data （as in this study） renders the difference – in – difference （DID）
method inapplicable （Wooldridge, 2010） . The ESR method accounts for
endogeneity by estimating a simultaneous equations model with endogenous
switching by full information maximum likelihood （FIML） . Although ESR
relies on the same normality assumptions as the instrumental variable methods, the approach is more efficient. By modeling both selection and outcome
equations, ESR has the advantage of controlling for observable and unobservable factors which affect the treatment itself and disentangle the factors influ-
encing the outcomes among treated and control groups. And FIML provides an
efficient method to estimate ESR models （Lokshin and Sajaia, 2004） .

6. 2. 2. 1 Endogenous Switching Regression

The application of the ESR method in this study involves two equations. The first utilizes the probit model, eq. （6 – 1）, to represent farmers' decisions to work off – farm, and the second, in contradistinction to
eq. （6 –2）, specifies two linear outcome equations （in our study, household welfare） for off – farm participant households and non – participant
households：

$$Y_{1i} = \beta_1 X_{1i} + \varepsilon_{1i,} \text{ if } L_i = 1 \qquad (6-3)$$

$$Y_{0i} = \beta_0 X_{0i} + \varepsilon_{0i,} \text{ if } L_i = 0 \qquad (6-4)$$

where the parameters are as defined for eq. （6 –2） .

As indicated in section 6. 2. 1, self－selection into off－farm employment (or not) may lead to correlation between the error terms of the selection eq. (6－1), and that in outcome eqs. (6－3) and (6－4), due to
some unobservable heterogeneity. The ESR framework assumes that the error
terms ε, ε_{1i} and ε_{0i} have a trivariate normal distribution with a mean of zero
and a nonzero covariance matrix:

$$\text{cov}(\mu_i, \varepsilon_1, \varepsilon_0) = \begin{bmatrix} \sigma_\mu^2 & \sigma_{\mu 1} & \sigma_{\mu 0} \\ \sigma_{1\mu} & \sigma_1^2 & \cdot \\ \sigma_{0\mu} & \cdot & \sigma_0^2 \end{bmatrix} \tag{6-5}$$

where $\sigma_\mu^2 = \text{var } (\mu_i)$, the variance of eq. (6－1), which can be assumed
to be equal to 1 since the coefficients are estimable only up to a scale factor;
$\sigma_1^2 = \text{var } (\varepsilon_1)$; $\sigma_0^2 = \text{var } (\varepsilon_0)$; $\sigma_{1\mu} = \text{cov } (\varepsilon_1, \mu_i)$; $\sigma_{0\mu} = \text{cov } (\varepsilon_0, \mu_i)$;
the covariance between ε_1 and ε_0, is not defined since the two states $L_i = 1$ and
$L_i = 0$ are not simultaneously observable (Maddala, 1983) .

In the presence of selection bias and conditional upon off－farm participation, the expected values of the error terms for off farm participant households in eq. (6－3) and non－participant households in eq. (6－4) will
be different from zero:

$$E(\varepsilon_{1i} \mid L_i = 1) = E(\varepsilon_{1i} \mid \mu_i > -Z_i\alpha) = \sigma_{1\mu}\left[\frac{\phi(Z_i\alpha)}{\Phi(Z_i\alpha)}\right] = \sigma_{1\mu}\lambda_{1i}$$

$$\tag{6-6}$$

$$E(\varepsilon_{0i} \mid L_i = 0) = E(\varepsilon_{0i} \mid \mu_i \leqslant -Z_i\alpha) = \sigma_{0\mu}\left[\frac{-\phi(Z_i\alpha)}{1 - \Phi(Z_i\alpha)}\right] = \sigma_{0\mu}\lambda_{0i}$$

$$\tag{6-7}$$

where ϕ (－) and Φ (－) are the probability density and cumulative dis-

◇ 退耕还林政策与黄土高原地区农户可持续生计：基于生产率和效率的实证研究
Grain for Green Program and Sustainable Agriculture and Rural Livelihoods of the Loess
Plateau in China: Empirical Studies with Measurement of Productivity and Efficiency

tribution functions of the standard normal distribution, respectively; and
$\left[\frac{\phi(Z_i\alpha)}{\Phi(Z_i\alpha)}\right] = \lambda_{1i}$ and $\left[\frac{-\phi(Z_i\alpha)}{1 - \Phi(Z_i\alpha)}\right] = \lambda_{0i}$ are referred to as the inverse Mills

ratio (IMR), which can be substituted into eqs. (6−3) and (6−4) to
control for sample selection bias. Significance of the estimated covariances
$\hat{\sigma}_{1\mu}$ and $\hat{\sigma}_{0\mu}$, and the correlation coefficients between the selection and outcome equations confirms the presence of sample selection bias.

6.2.2.2 Treatment Effect of Off−farm Employment on Household Welfare

It is necessary to estimate the treatment effect of participation in off−
farm work on household welfare to correct the selection bias. The ESR method can be used to derive consistent conditional expectations, which are used
to compute counterfactual and actual (observed) outcomes for off−farm
participant households and non−participant households (Lokshin and Sajaia, 2004). Counterfactual outcomes refer to expected outcomes for off−
farm participant households had they not participated and for non−partici-
pant households had they participated. Conditional expectations for the different outcome scenarios are derived as follows (Maddala, 1983):

$$E(y_{1i} \mid L_i = 1) = X_{1i}\beta_1 + \sigma_{1\mu}\lambda_{1i} \qquad (6-8)$$

$$E(y_{0i} \mid L_i = 0) = X_{0i}\beta_0 + \sigma_{0\mu}\lambda_{0i} \qquad (6-9)$$

$$E(y_{0i} \mid L_i = 1) = X_{1i}\beta_0 + \sigma_{0\mu}\lambda_{1i} \qquad (6-10)$$

$$E(y_{1i} \mid L_i = 0) = X_{0i}\beta_1 + \sigma_{1\mu}\lambda_{0i} \qquad (6-11)$$

Eqs. (6−8) and (6−9) are observed outcomes conditional on off−
farm participation and non−participation, respectively. Eq. (6−10) is
the expected outcome for off−farm participant households had they not participated in off−farm work, which is the counterfactual outcome for off−farm

participant households. Eq. （6 – 11） is the expected outcome for non – participant households had they participated in off – farm work, and it also serves as the counterfactual outcome for non – participant households.

Following Heckman et al. （2001）, the average treatment effect on the treated （ATT） is the difference between the outcomes in eqs. （6 – 8） and （6 – 10）, which represents the welfare effect of off – farm participation of the households that actually participated in off – farm work; Similarly, the average treatment effect on the untreated （ATU） for non – participant households, can be calculated as the difference between eqs. （6 – 9） and （6 – 11）:

$$ATT = E(y_{1i} \mid L_i = 1) - E(y_{0i} \mid L_i = 1) = X_{1i}(\beta_1 - \beta_0) + (\sigma_{1\mu} - \sigma_{0\mu})\lambda_{1i}$$

$$(6 - 12)$$

$$ATU = E(y_{1i} \mid L_i = 0) - E(y_{0i} \mid L_i = 0) = X_{0i}(\beta_1 - \beta_0) + (\sigma_{1\mu} - \sigma_{0\mu})\lambda_{0i}$$

$$(6 - 13)$$

Heterogeneity effects can also be estimated. This is important since non – participant households may experience lower household welfare than off – farm participant households due to some unobservable characteristics. To re- flect this, a base heterogeneity （BH） effect is defined as the difference be- tween eqs. （6 – 8） and （6 – 11） for off – farm participation, and the difference between eqs. （6 – 10） and （6 – 9） for non – participation:

$$BH_1 = E(y_{1i} \mid L_i = 1) - E(y_{1i} \mid L_i = 0) = (X_{1i} - X_{0i})\beta_1 + \sigma_{1\mu}(\lambda_{1i} - \lambda_{0i})$$

$$(6 - 14)$$

$$BH_0 = E(y_{0i} \mid L_i = 1) - E(y_{0i} \mid L_i = 0) = (X_{1i} - X_{0i})\beta_0 + \sigma_{0\mu}(\lambda_{1i} - \lambda_{0i})$$

$$(6 - 15)$$

To investigate whether the effect of off – farm participation on household welfare is larger or smaller for farmers that participated in off – farm work

◇ 退耕还林政策与黄土高原地区农户可持续生计：基于生产率和效率的实证研究
Grain for Green Program and Sustainable Agriculture and Rural Livelihoods of the Loess
Plateau in China: Empirical Studies with Measurement of Productivity and Efficiency

had they not participated, or for farmers that did not participate in off – farm work had they participated, requires computation of transitional heterogeneity (TH) effects. The TH effect is equal to the difference between BH_1 and BH_0 or the difference between ATT and ATU.

6.3　Model and Data

6.3.1　Empirical Model Specification

Household welfare and well – being indicators are generally relevant to farm and household income, consumption expenditure and food security (Baležentis et al., 2011). In the absence of any direct indicators of household expenditure, we take three variables into account: *Household_ income*, *Per_ capita_ household_ income* and *Farm_ productivity*, which have all been used previously as indirect indicators of household welfare (Holden et al., 2004; Kuntashula and Mungatana, 2013; Alem et al., 2015). Total household income consists of farm and off – farm income, and farm productivity in our study refers to labor productivity, which is calculated by dividing farm income by number of household members working on farm.

The selection of explanatory variables that are believed to have an impact on the capacity or motivation of farm households to participate in off – farm work and on their household welfare is mainly based on previous studies (e. g., Feder et al., 1990; Ahearn et al., 2006; Beyene, 2008; El – Osta et al., 2008; Oseni and Winters, 2009). We chose *Education*, *Child* and *Land/labor*, *Conservation_ payments*, *Tenancy*, *Credit*, and

Extension_ services. The definition of *Child*, *Land/labor*, *Conservation_ payments*, *Tenancy*, *Credit*, and *Extension_ services* is the same as in previous studies. Here since we are interested in the factors that affect household welfare, the *Education* variable in this study is measured as the proportion of household members who have completed secondary education.

6. 3. 2　Descriptive Statistics of the Data

This study involves 225 households. Table 6 – 1 gives a description of the data. Overall, 90. 2% (203) of households had family members participating in off – farm work. The table also presents summary statistics and mean difference test results between off – farm participant households and non – participant households for all variables used in the analysis. There are some notable differences in characteristics between off – farm participant households and non – participant households: off – farm participant households were generally better – educated, much closer to the nearest central labor market (Yan' an City) and less likely to have children in the family while non – participant households tended to have better access to agricultural extension services. For the household welfare variables, off – farm participant households had higher household income and per capita household income and lower farm productivity on average, but the mean differences in these outcome variables between off – farm participant and non – participant households were not statistically significant. Although the comparison highlights some significant differences between the two groups of households, it is important to note that these descriptive statistics represent only simple mean comparisons and do not take into account issues such as selection bias, which will be addressed in the following analysis.

◇ 退耕还林政策与黄土高原地区农户可持续生计：基于生产率和效率的实证研究

Grain for Green Program and Sustainable Agriculture and Rural Livelihoods of the Loess Plateau in China: Empirical Studies with Measurement of Productivity and Efficiency

Table 6 – 1 Comparative Statistics of Variables between Households of Off – farm Employment Participant and Non – participant

Variables	Total Sample		Participant		Non – participant		Difference
	Mean	SD	Mean	SD	Mean	SD	
Outcome Variables							
Household_ income (thousand yuan)	15. 315	0. 961	15. 339	0. 913	15. 094	5. 107	0. 246
Per _ capita _ household _ income (thousand yuan/person)	6. 502	0. 378	6. 519	0. 355	6. 345	2. 350	0. 174
Farm _ productivity (thousand yuan/person)	6. 068	8. 479	5. 962	8. 148	7. 046	9. 617	– 1. 084
Explanatory Variables							
Conservation _ payments (thousand yuan)	3. 905	3. 221	3. 927	2. 322	3. 702	7. 662	0. 225
Tenancy (%)	0. 030	0. 146	0. 015	0. 006	0. 168	0. 071	– 0. 153
Credit (%)	0. 038	0. 276	0. 034	0. 282	0. 071	0. 180	– 0. 036
Extension_ services (0/1)	0. 160	0. 363	0. 127	0. 329	0. 465	0. 510	– 0. 338 ***
Education (%)	0. 287	0. 375	0. 301	0. 380	0. 158	0. 295	0. 143 **
Child (0/1)	0. 210	0. 407	0. 188	0. 391	0. 413	0. 503	– 0. 222 **
Land/labor (mu/person)	4. 296	2. 813	4. 209	2. 702	5. 099	3. 634	– 0. 890
Instrument							
Distance (kilometers)	56. 809	28. 338	52. 276	24. 692	98. 640	25. 874	– 46. 361 ***
Total Sample	225		203		22		

Note: The symbols *, **, *** indicate statistical significance at the 1%, 5%, and 10% levels, respectively.

6. 4 Results and Discussions

Proper identification in the ESR method requires that at least one variable in Z is omitted from X (Lokshin and Sajaia, 2004). To save space, the result of model test was omitted. Please refer to Li et al. (2019) for details. We used the Stata "movestay" command to estimate the ESR models with the FIML estimator (Lokshin and Sajaia, 2004). Table 6 – 2 presents results from the ESR models.

6.4.1 Determinants of Household Members' Off – farm Participation

Column 1 reports results for off – farm work participation from the selection equation of the household income model (Table 6 – 2).

Table 6 – 2 ESR Estimate for Off – farm Employment Participation and Household Welfare

	Household_ income			Per_ capita_ household_ income		Farm_ productivity	
	(1)	(2)	(3)	(4)	(5)	(6)	(7)
	Participation(1/0)	1	0	1	0	1	0
Education	2.029 **	0.783 ***	0.274	0.609 ***	-0.495	2.499 **	28.045 **
Child	-0.811 **	-0.301 ***	-0.542 **	-0.470 ***	-0.922 ***	-0.595 *	-5.565 *
Land/labor	-0.191 **	-0.056 ***	-0.000	0.009	0.105	-0.142	0.329
Conservation _ payments	0.285	-0.214 ***	0.048	-0.206 ***	-0.265	-1.580 *	1.366
Tenancy	-2.169	-0.106	1.486 *	0.196	0.066	19.394 ***	36.618 ***
Credit	-0.485	0.269 **	-0.539	0.204 *	0.146	1.848 *	0.079
Extension_ services	0.542	0.612 ***	0.948 ***	0.339 ***	0.713 ***	10.481 ***	8.664 **
Distance	-0.035 ***						
Intercept	2.497	11.017 ***	8.606 ***	9.910 ***	7.821 ***	15.471 **	-2.457
$\ln\sigma_1$		-0.676 ***		-0.804 ***		1.802 ***	
$\ln\sigma_0$			-0.410 **		-0.955 ***		2.132 ***
ρ_1		0.184		0.258		-0.042	
ρ_0			0.334 *		0.760 *		0.330 *
LR test of indep. eqns.	3.93 **			3.69 **		0.62 *	

Note: A. Off – farm participation is labelled 1 for participating households and 0 for those that did not participate. Statistics σ_1 and σ_0 denote the square – root of the variance of the error terms ε_{1i}, ε_{0i} in outcome eqs. (6 – 3) and (6 – 4), respectively while ρ_1 and ρ_2 denote the correlation coefficients between the error term μ_i of the selection equation (6 – 1) and the error terms ε_{1i}, ε_{0i} of outcome eqs. (6 – 3) and (6 – 4), respectively.

B. The symbols *, **, *** indicate statistical significance at the 1%, 5%, and 10% levels, respectively.

◇ 退耕还林政策与黄土高原地区农户可持续生计：基于生产率和效率的实证研究
Grain for Green Program and Sustainable Agriculture and Rural Livelihoods of the Loess
Plateau in China: Empirical Studies with Measurement of Productivity and Efficiency

The positive relationship between household educational attainment and off – farm participation is consistent with previous studies (e. g. , Liu, 2017) . People with higher educational levels are generally more knowledge-able about employment opportunities, more adaptable to a range of tasks, more ready to acquire new skills, and more likely to gain off – farm wage employment (Welch, 1970; Appleton and Balihuta, 1996; Beyene, 2008; Fan et al. , 2018) .

Due to imperfections in rural labor markets, an increase in the land re-source endowment will increase the reservation wage of household members and decrease their participation in off – farm work. Alternatively, a shortage of land resources should motivate them to diversify their livelihoods, inclu-ding off – farm employment (Beyene, 2008) . This might account for the negative relationship between land resource endowment and off – farm partic-ipation.

In line with our expectations, the presence of children in the family de-creases the likelihood of off – farm job participation. Chinese famers who choose to work in the city typically do not take their children with them due to the high cost of living and urban schooling. For this reason, most farmers with children prefer on – farm work so they can take care of the children at the same time (Liang et al. , 2012) .

It is important to note that government conservation payments (*Conser-vation_ payments*) had no significant impact on the participation of house-holds in off – farm work. Households that participated in GfG increasingly shifted their labor endowment from on – farm work to the off – farm labor market (Xie et al. , 2006; Uchida et al. , 2009; Xu et al. , 2010; Yao et al. , 2010) . This could come as a result of the substitution effect that is triggered by the labor made surplus by the program seeking more remunerative activities (Uchida et al. , 2007; Liang et al. , 2012) . However, this does not necessarily mean that the conservation payments have the expected liquidity relaxation effect on the participating households. Using rigorous effect evaluation method like PSM and DID, Uchida et al. (2007) found very weak evidence of off – farm participation prompted by the program and asserted that time is needed to induce large changes. In a subsequent study (Uchida et al. , 2009), they observed an increase in off – farm labor participation induced by the program but with an impact that would only be significant in households that were liquidity constrained or that had a certain level of educational attainment. Work by Liang et al. (2012) supports the wealth effect, with conservation payments causing a decrease in the supply of household labor in both on – farm and migrant work (one kind of off – farm activities) . In contrast to their findings, our results are more nuanced in that neither an increase nor a decrease in conservation payments would significantly affect household decisions about off – farm participation. However, our results do support their view of the importance of human capital and household composition (Uchida et al. , 2007; Uchida et al. , 2009; Liang et al. , 2012) in facilitating (or impeding) off – farm participation.

6. 4. 2　Determinants of Household Welfare in the Setting of GfG

The estimate for the welfare outcome equations suggests notable differences in the variables for off – farm participant households and non – participant households. Such differences highlight again the possibility that the two groups of farmers are potentially different in several characteristics (selection bias) and justify the use of the ESR model instead of pooling the data

◇ 退耕还林政策与黄土高原地区农户可持续生计：基于生产率和效率的实证研究
Grain for Green Program and Sustainable Agriculture and Rural Livelihoods of the Loess
Plateau in China: Empirical Studies with Measurement of Productivity and Efficiency

into a single equation.

The results indicate that government conservation payments (*Conservation_ payments*) are significantly and negatively related to household income, per capita household income and farm productivity for off – farm participant households. Government conservation payments from GfG may induce changes in labor and land reallocation with the liquidity effect and contribute to improving household welfare for the households participating in the program. But resembling the characteristics of decoupled subsidies, conservation payments may also cause a wealth effect that allows farmers to work less while maintaining consumption levels (Ahearn et al., 2006; El – Osta et al., 2008; Donnellan and Hennessy, 2012). While neither the liquidity effect nor the wealth effect was detected for the whole sample based on the result of off – farm participation, the result of the significant negative relationship between conservation payments and household welfare indicators might still suggest that the wealth effect prevails for the off – farm participant households. Increasing the amount of conservation payments to households will only dissuade them from exerting more effort in farm and/or off – farm activities, causing a decrease in farm productivity, household income and per capita household income. In contrast, conservation payments are not significantly related to household welfare indicators for off – farm non – participant households. In other words, neither the wealth effect nor the liquidity effect is evident for these households based on the results of the welfare outcome equations. As observed in field work and partly verified in section 6. 4. 1, non – participant households fall into two sub – groups: intensive producers (e. g., greenhouse horticulture) and those with family care obligations or those which are incompetent (elderly, disabled, or illiterate) to work in off - farm occupations. These last non - participants were mostly poor households engaged in traditional farming practices. Due to the small sample size, it would be difficult to disentangle these sub - groups, however, the results suggest that conservation payments would relax the liquidity con- straints on these poor households, compared with their off - farm participant counterparts.

For the other variables, consistent with previous studies (e. g. , Liang et al. , 2012; Alem et al. , 2015), providing extension services (*Exten- sion_ services*) significantly and positively affect household welfare for all three indicators and the presence of children in the family (*Child*) signifi- cantly and negatively affect household welfare. In line with our expectations, access to credit (*Credit*) and the educational attainment of the households (*Education*) are significantly and positively related to all household welfare indicators, and land resource endowment (*Land/labor*) is significantly and negatively related to household income, for off - farm participant house- holds. One possible reason for the insignificance of these variables for non - participant households may be the small sample size of this group which makes it difficult to attain statistical significance. Of note, access of farm households to the land rental market (*Tenancy*) is significantly and positively related to farm productivity for both off - farm participant and non - participant house- holds, and significantly improves household income for non - participant households. One possible explanation is that farm households with higher re- turns to land and thus higher farm productivity have greater incentive to in- vest in more land.

◇ 退耕还林政策与黄土高原地区农户可持续生计：基于生产率和效率的实证研究

Grain for Green Program and Sustainable Agriculture and Rural Livelihoods of the Loess Plateau in China: Empirical Studies with Measurement of Productivity and Efficiency

6.4.3 Impact of Off – farm Employment on Household Welfare

Table 6 – 3 shows the expected household income, per capita household income, and farm productivity for both off – farm participant and non – participant households under actual and counterfactual scenarios, and presents the selection bias – corrected estimate results of the welfare impact of off – farm participation.

Table 6 – 3 Impacts of Off – farm Employment on Household Welfare:

Treatment and Heterogeneity Effects

Outcome Variable	Sub – sample	Decision Stage				Treatment Effects	
			To Participate		Not – to – participate	(ATT – ATU)	
Household_ income	Participant	(a)	9.333	(c)	9.030	ATT	0.303 ***
	Non – participant	(d)	9.307	(b)	9.061	ATU	0.246 *
	Heterogeneous effects	(e)	0.026	(f)	– 0.031	TH	0.057
Per_ capita_ household_ income	Participant	(a)	8.538	(c)	7.781	ATT	0.757 ***
	Non – participant	(d)	8.526	(b)	8.400	ATU	0.126 *
	Heterogeneous effects	(e)	0.012	(f)	– 0.619 ***	TH	0.631 ***
Farm_ Productivity	Participant	(a)	5.962	(c)	7.112	ATT	– 1.150 ***
	Non – participant	(d)	6.175	(b)	7.046	ATU	– 0.871 **
	Heterogeneous effects	(e)	– 0.213 ***	(f)	0.066	TH	– 0.279 ***

Note: The symbols *, **, *** indicate statistical significance at the 1%, 5%, and 10% levels, respectively.

For off – farm participant households, estimate results on ATT suggest that participation generates significantly higher household income and per capita household income compared with what they would have received under a no participation scenario. On average, off – farm participant households increased their household income by 3.2% and their per capita household income by 8. 9% (as shown by the difference in the logarithms of the dependent variables), while farm labor productivity was reduced by 19. 3%. This result implies that the marginal productivity of labor is still much lower on – farm than off – farm, and participating in off – farm work is beneficial for improving the economic status for farmers on the Loess Plateau, even though it has an adverse impact on farm production. Reardon et al. (1994) have proposed a theoretical framework showing that off – farm activities may compete with farm activities for labor and other resources, and it may also contribute to reinvestment of higher profits in the farm. Off – farm work generally draws physically stronger and better educated labor away from the farm (Rozelle et al. , 1999) but due to imperfections in rural labor markets, this cannot be replaced with labor of equivalent quality from local rural sources. This lost labor effect has often been found to have an adverse impact on farm productivity and decreased farm production in the developing countries (Davis et al. , 2009; Shi, 2018) .

Similar results were found for non – participant households, only that the impact of off – farm participation is not as significant on household income and per capita household income (significant at the 10% level) . On average, off – farm participation would decrease farm productivity by 14. 1% and increase household income by 2. 6% and per capita household income by 1. 4%.

As discussed in section 6. 2. 2. 2, transitional heterogeneity (TH) measures whether the welfare effect of off – farm participation is larger or smaller for off – farm participant households had they not participated, or for non – participant households had they participated. The significantly positive TH on per capita household income and significantly negative TH on farm

◇ 退耕还林政策与黄土高原地区农户可持续生计：基于生产率和效率的实证研究
Grain for Green Program and Sustainable Agriculture and Rural Livelihoods of the Loess
Plateau in China： Empirical Studies with Measurement of Productivity and Efficiency

productivity indicate that off – farm participant households benefit signifi-cantly more on per capita household income and lose more on farm productivi-ty, than those non – participant counterpart households. The differences in the welfare effect of off – farm participation between off – farm participant households and non – participant households are explained mainly by the sig-nificant base heterogeneity between the two groups as indicated by (e) and (f) in Table 6 – 3.

Generally speaking, the findings indicate that due to rural labor market imperfections, participation in off – farm work competes with farm activities for labor resources, which leads to a decrease in on – farm human capital and labor productivity (see also Huang et al., 2010; Shi, 2018). The lost la-bor and the decreasing labor productivity on farm production would lead to de-creased farm output and farm income. Nevertheless, given that off – farm work is still generally more lucrative than farm activities, participation in off – farm work would still alleviate rural poverty in China. In response to concerns about food security due to the decreased farm production, we can address the factors that would help farm households to increase their farm productivi-ty based on results from section 6.4.2. For example, delivering more agri-cultural extension services to farm households, facilitating their access to the land rental market, improving their educational attainment, or improving rural childcare arrangements would help them improve their farm productivity.

6. 5　Conclusions

Conservation payments are provided for participating farmers in GfG for conserving sloping or marginal land. The payments were expected to induce land and labor reallocation, therefore contribute to environmental rehabilitation and poverty alleviation. Among the rest, off – farm participation has the potential to play a crucial role in alleviating poverty and improving household welfare. The aim of this study is therefore to examine the factors (including conservation payments) that influence the household's decision to participate in off – farm work and estimate the impact of off – farm participation on household welfare under the auspices of GfG. Using an ESR model estimated simultaneously, we accounted for selection bias and endogeneity problems. This is important in farm smallholder settings where farmers make decisions on labor allocation and other production activities simultaneously, and some observable and unobservable characteristics might affect both off – farm participation and their household welfare.

The results suggest that off – farm participation significantly increased household income and per capita household income, and significantly decreased farm productivity for both off – farm participant and non – participant households. This not only suggests that participation in off – farm work is still an effective way to alleviate poverty for rural households, but also cautions that off – farm work competes with farm work for labor with imperfections in rural labor markets, which might be detrimental to agricultural production. Remittances received from out – migrant family members should provide

◇ 退耕还林政策与黄土高原地区农户可持续生计：基于生产率和效率的实证研究
Grain for Green Program and Sustainable Agriculture and Rural Livelihoods of the Loess
Plateau in China: Empirical Studies with Measurement of Productivity and Efficiency

an effective way to outbreak farms' capital constraints and contribute to agricultural production. But still the labor mobility by rural – urban migration in China is subject to significant institutional constraints due to the different household registration system (so called "hukou" in Chinese) between rural and urban residents and thus different social welfares. In this setting, it is difficult for the peasant worker to have savings and remittances to send back to their families.

Household characteristics, conservation payments and other institutional variables affect household participation in off – farm work and have heterogeneous effects on welfare outcomes between participant and non – participant households. Among other explanatory factors, human capital (to be specific in this study, educational attainment of the household) and household composition (presence of children) have an obvious impact on both off – farm participation and household welfare. Other important factors include land resource endowment of the household, access to the land rental market, credit market, and extension services.

As one of the most important measures in GfG, conservation payments show no significant impact on households' off – farm participation and household welfare for off – farm non – participants, but have a significantly negative impact on household welfare for off – farm participant households. This result might suggest a possible wealth effect upon off – farm participant households which demotivates them from exerting their efforts in farm and/or off – farm activities. The insignificant impact on non – participant households, however, might suggest that conservation payments relax the liquidity constraint on these poor households, compared with their off – farm participant counterparts.

This study carries important policy implications nevertheless. First, better targeting of poorer households, those challenged by childcare obligations, or illiteracy is needed to fulfill GfG mandate. Second, instead of throwing huge amounts of money into subsidizing farm households for conserving the land, greater emphasis should be placed on facilitating off – farm job participation and magnifying its impact on household welfare. Third, the results indicate that greater attention to the challenge of improved farm productivity is required for the sake of food security. And finally, the implications suggest an alternative agricultural policy orientation that includes better childcare arrangements; education, training, extension services, and other human capital increasing initiatives; improved transportation infrastructure; and improving and facilitating access to land, labor, and credit markets for smallholders.

Chapter 7 Farm – household Technical Efficiency and Its Determinant Factors

7. 1 Specific Objectives

The payments made by conservation programs in the developing countries are generally provided by the government (Wunder et al. , 2008),
which means they are typically made for a fixed term due to budget constraints. Unless farm householders are able to shift their agricultural practices
and other income – generating – activities with the relaxation of their liquidity
constraints to generate sustainable livelihoods, the programs won't succeed
(Wunder et al. , 2008; Grosjean and Kontoleon, 2009; Uchida et al. ,
2009) . For a farmland set – aside program like GfG in China, the sustainability or success of the program was widely acknowledged to be dependent
upon its ability to improve agricultural productivity and/or to enable households to access alternative employment opportunities (Xu et al. , 2004;
Uchida et al. , 2007; Xu et al. , 2010) . Households are less likely to
cultivate sloping land, which has a much lower marginal productivity of labor, if the output of the remaining farmland improves (Deng et al. , 2006)

or they have access to more attractive off – farm jobs (Groom et al. , 2010) so that the improved income can offset the loss of agricultural output from the set – aside land.

In the previous Chapters, we have found that a shift of the labor force toward off – farm employment (consistent with the majority of previous studies, e. g. , Uchida et al. , 2009; Groom et al. , 2010; Yao et al. , 2010; Kelly and Huo, 2013; Yin et al. , 2014; Zhen et al. , 2014), and that the income from off – farm employment help contribute to improved household income. However according to our study, participating in off – farm employment is very likely to adversely affect agricultural production. Due to the intricate relationship between farm and off – farm activities (Chikwama, 2004; Pfeiffer et al. , 2009), we think that emphasizing one aspect and neglecting the other might lead to an incomplete or misleading understanding of the program's effectiveness, especially in the case off – farm employment competes with on – farm activities and leads to reduced agricultural production (Holden et al. , 2004) . In addition, rising household income does not necessarily guarantee a sustainable or long – term livelihood (Scoones, 1998), which casts doubt upon the efficacy of longer – term mechanisms. Furthermore, the effectiveness of the program requires a more nuanced understanding of the poor households that it targets (Groom et al. , 2010) .

Farm household level technical efficiency is a newly developed concept (Chavas et al. , 2005) that is getting increasing recognition in the empirical literature (e. g. , Fletschner, 2008; Masters and Shively, 2010) . By extending traditional technical efficiency analysis at the farm level to the household level, this method considers the impact of farm household deci-

◇ 退耕还林政策与黄土高原地区农户可持续生计：基于生产率和效率的实证研究
Grain for Green Program and Sustainable Agriculture and Rural Livelihoods of the Loess
Plateau in China: Empirical Studies with Measurement of Productivity and Efficiency

sions on general household production activities, including farm production and off – farm employment. In a land set – aside program like GfG, a household level technical efficiency analysis provides important information on the performance of the households' use of its available technology and resources, including labor, capital and the remaining farm land to maximize its household income, indicative of the sustainability of its livelihood (Scoones, 1998). Therefore, the objective of the present study is to estimate the technical efficiency of households participating in GfG and to explore the determinant factors empirically. By regressing conservation payments from the program, which serve as the major program measure, and other factors on household technical efficiency with a traditional OLS regression analysis, this study identifies the effect of the program on sustainable livelihoods of the farm households, and the constraints that prevent their optimal use of household resources and technologies for a more sustainable livelihood. In addition, a quantile regression analysis is also deployed to explore the possible heterogeneous effect of the conservation payments on the technical efficiency of different household groups. The results of this analysis will provide an empirical basis for improvements to GfG program policies and targeting of farm households.

7.2　Methods

7.2.1　Household Technical Efficiency Estimation

Chavas et al. (2005) has demonstrated that in the developing countries, there is jointness in the technologies underlying farm and nonfarm activities (or non – separability between farm household production and consumption decisions) due to market failures. Accordingly, they developed a method for measuring household level technical efficiency which included off – farm activities in the traditional farm efficiency estimation framework.

Following their work, we first develop a model of the household decision process. Suppose M family members in a farm household make production, consumption, and labor allocation decisions jointly for a specific time – period, and that they maximize utility U subject to budget and time constraints. Thus the household decision process can be modeled as:

Maximize $U = U\ (z,\ l)$, $\qquad\qquad\qquad\qquad\qquad\qquad$ (7 – 1)

s. t.

$q'z \leqslant p'y - r'x + N$

$T_m = F_m + L_m + l_m$, $m = 1,\ 2,\ \cdots,\ M,\ (x,\ F,\ H,\ L;\ y,\ N)\ \in X$

where l denotes household service; q' denotes price vectors for consumption goods z; p' denotes price vectors for farm outputs y; r' denotes price vectors for non – labor inputs x; N denotes off – farm income; T_m denotes the total amount of time available to the mth family member; F_m denotes the amount of time working on the farm for the mth family member; L_m denotes the amount of time working off – farm for the mth family member; l_m denotes the amount of time for household service for the mth family member; X denotes the technology the household is facing, and $(x,\ F,\ L;\ y,\ N)\ \in X$ means outputs $(y,\ N)$ can be feasibly produced with inputs $(x,\ F,\ L)$ under technology X.

Families differ in the extent to which they are willing to substitute household services for consumption goods, but for any given level of house-

◇ 退耕还林政策与黄土高原地区农户可持续生计：基于生产率和效率的实证研究

Grain for Green Program and Sustainable Agriculture and Rural Livelihoods of the Loess Plateau in China: Empirical Studies with Measurement of Productivity and Efficiency

hold services l, nonsatiation of the utility function implies that household will maximize its consumption, which is in turn equivalent to maximizing its profit conditional on l:

$$\pi(p, \ r, \ T-l) = \mathrm{Max}(p'y - r'x + N) \tag{7-2}$$

s. t.

$$F_m + L_m = T_m - l_m, \ m = 1, \ 2, \ \cdots, \ M, \ (x, \ F, \ L; \ y, \ N) \in X$$

The profit maximization problem in equation (7-2) is equivalent to the revenue maximization problem conditional on inputs $(x, \ F, \ L)$

$$\tau(p, \ x, \ F, \ L, \ X) = \mathrm{Max}_{y,N}\{p'y + N : (x, \ F, \ L; \ y, \ N) \in X\}$$

$$\tag{7-3}$$

If a household produces as much as is feasible given its resources, the technology available, and the level of household services provided, it will be technically efficient. All the efficient households constitute the production possibility frontier, and the technical efficiency of each household can be calculated according to its distance to that frontier.

We still use DEA to estimate technical efficiency, the same reason as specified in previous studies. The linear programming was omitted to save space.

7.2.2　Second-stage Regression Analysis

We chose OLS model the same reason as specified in section 5.2.2.

7. 3   Model and Data

7. 3. 1   Inputs and Outputs for Household Efficiency Estimation and the Explanatory Variables

The estimation of household – level technical efficiency involves the following data: two outputs including *Farm income* and *Off – farm income*; four inputs including *Farm labor* and *Off – farm labor*, both measured in worker – months; *Land*, *Materials and capital*, are defined the same way as in previous studies.

We incorporated the following variables in our second – stage regression model based on previous studies (e. g. , Matshe and Young, 2004; Fletschner, 2008; El – Osta et al. , 2008; Solís et al. , 2009): *Education*, *Child*, *Land/labor*, *Conservation _ payments*, *Tenancy*, *Credit*, and *Extension_ services*. All the definitions are the same as in the previous study. Except for *Child*, other variables are assumed to be positively related to household efficiency.

7. 3. 2   Descriptive Statistics of the Data

Table 7 – 1 presents descriptive statistics of the input and output variables to be included in the DEA model to estimate household technical efficiencies and the variables that are expected to affect household technical efficiencies for the 225 farm households.

◇ 退耕还林政策与黄土高原地区农户可持续生计：基于生产率和效率的实证研究

Grain for Green Program and Sustainable Agriculture and Rural Livelihoods of the Loess Plateau in China: Empirical Studies with Measurement of Productivity and Efficiency

Table 7 – 1   Descriptive Statistics of Variables Used for Household

Efficiency Estimation and Econometric Models

	Variables	Mean	SD	Min	Max
Outputs	*Farm income* (thousand yuan)	6. 068	11. 479	0. 119	72. 760
	Off – farm income (thousand yuan)	9. 246	7. 795	0. 000	48. 800
Inputs	*Land* (mu)	8. 585	4. 966	0. 800	30. 000
	Farm labor (person)	1. 407	0. 633	0. 400	4. 000
	Off – farm labor (person)	0. 931	0. 583	0. 000	3. 000
	Materials and capital (thousand yuan)	0. 840	1. 290	0. 033	12. 340
Explanatory Variables	*Education* (%)	0. 287	0. 376	0. 000	1. 000
	Child	0. 210	0. 407	0. 000	1. 000
	Land/labor	4. 296	2. 813	0. 267	15. 000
	Conservation_ payments	3. 905	3. 221	0. 640	37. 180
	Tenancy	0. 030	0. 146	0. 000	1. 000
	Credit (0/1)	0. 038	0. 276	0. 000	3. 884
	Extension_ services (0/1)	0. 160	0. 363	0. 000	1. 000

For the labor force, 60. 3% of their working time allocated to farm work, and 39. 7% allocated to off – farm work, however the proportion of farm income to household income (subsidy excluded) was only 39. 5%, while off – farm income amounted to 60. 5%. This suggests a general much higher return to off – farm works than on – farm works. Government conservation payments to rural households amounted to 3. 90 thousand Yuan on average, a large proportion to total household income. In contrast, few of the households had access to rented farmland, extension services, or credit. The land endowment seems adequate with cultivated land of 4. 3 mu per capita (compared with the value of around 1. 5 mu per capita nationwide), 21% of the households had children, and the average educational level for the householders was low, with only 30% of the household members had

completed secondary education. And we should also note that substantial variance exists in the sample households.

7. 4   Results and Discussions

7. 4. 1   Household Technical Efficiency

Descriptive statistics and frequency distribution of the efficiency scores
at the household level were put forward in Table 7 – 2 and Figure 7 – 1. The
mean VRSTE of the sample households is 0. 669, which means the farm
households could decrease their inputs by 33. 1% and still generate the same
amount of farm and off – farm income. And here we should note that substantial variation exists in technical efficiencies for the sample households (SD
of 0. 209) . The distribution shows that 176 (78. 2%) of households had
technical efficiency scores larger than 0. 5, with 44 (19. 6%) of them
technically efficient.

Table 7 – 2   Descriptive Statistics of Technical Efficiencies and the

Nature of Returns – to – Scale

Item	CRSTE	VRSTE	SE
Mean	0. 382	0. 669	0. 555
SD	0. 253	0. 209	0. 250
Min	0. 034	0. 299	0. 097
Max	1. 000	1. 000	1. 000
IRS (%)	192 (85. 3)		
DRS (%)	20 (8. 9)		
MPSS (%)	13 (5. 8)		

◆ 退耕还林政策与黄土高原地区农户可持续生计：基于生产率和效率的实证研究
Grain for Green Program and Sustainable Agriculture and Rural Livelihoods of the Loess
Plateau in China: Empirical Studies with Measurement of Productivity and Efficiency

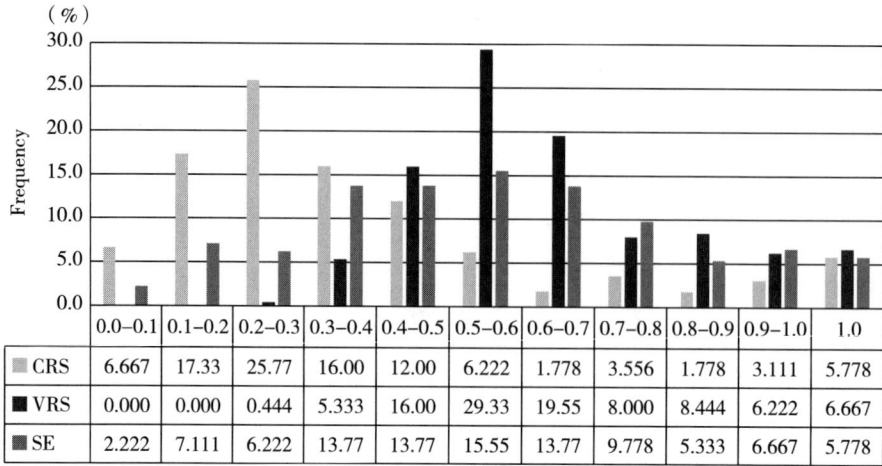

	0.0–0.1	0.1–0.2	0.2–0.3	0.3–0.4	0.4–0.5	0.5–0.6	0.6–0.7	0.7–0.8	0.8–0.9	0.9–1.0	1.0
CRS	6.667	17.33	25.77	16.00	12.00	6.222	1.778	3.556	1.778	3.111	5.778
VRS	0.000	0.000	0.444	5.333	16.00	29.33	19.55	8.000	8.444	6.222	6.667
SE	2.222	7.111	6.222	13.77	13.77	15.55	13.77	9.778	5.333	6.667	5.778

Figure 7 – 1   Frequency Distribution of Household Efficiencies

We also checked the status of scale efficiency and the nature of returns to scale of households. The result in Table 7 – 2 shows that the average scale efficiency for the households was 0. 555, indicating the main source of technical inefficiency for the sample households are due more to inappropriate scales. Only 18 (15. 6%) of sample households are scale efficient, among which 5 (2. 2%) are under the most productive scale size and 13 (5. 7%) are with constant return to scale. The remainder (207 or 92. 0%) of them was scale inefficient, mostly under increasing returns to scale (163 or 72. 4%). The finding of increasing returns to scales is consistent with our study including only farm activities (Chapter 4). For these households, their operating scales were too small and expanding their land, labor and capital resources proportionally would lead to a proportionally larger household income.

7. 4. 2   Determinants of Farm Household Technical Efficiency

The results of the regression analysis of the explanatory variables on

household technical efficiencies (VRSTE) generated from STATA are reported in Table 7 – 3, with the result from OLS regression in column1, sequence quantile regression estimation for the 0. 40, 0. 60, and 0. 80 quantiles of the farm household technical efficiency score distribution, and tests
for equality of coefficients across quantiles, in column 2, 3, 4 and 5, respectively (we used the Stata sqreg command to generate the quantile regression analysis result).

Table 7 – 3　OLS and Quantile Regression Analysis of the Explanatory

Variables on Household Technical Efficiencies

	OLS		Quantile Regression		
	(1)　TE	(2)　Q40	(3)　Q60	(4)　Q80	(5)　Wald test　(p)
Constant	1. 365 ***	1. 004 ***	1. 164 ***	1. 552 ***	0. 008
Education	0. 003	0. 062	0. 064 *	0. 071 *	0. 574
Child	-0. 131 ***	-0. 083 **	-0. 108 **	-0. 168 **	0. 059
Land/labor	-0. 003	-0. 003	-0. 005	-0. 009	0. 156
Conservation_ payments	-0. 190 **	-0. 119	-0. 137 *	-0. 178 *	0. 046
Tenancy	0. 265 *	0. 315	0. 193	0. 103	0. 368
Credit	0. 068 *	0. 094	0. 775 **	0. 385 **	0. 158
Extension_ services	0. 017	0. 081 *	0. 098	0. 139	0. 021

Note: The symbols *, **, *** indicate statistical significance at the 1%, 5%, and 10% levels, respectively.

According to the result of OLS regression, the conservation payments to
the households (Conservation_ payments) and presence of children in the
family (Child) were negatively related to household technical efficiency,
while the access to credit (Credit) and land rental market (Tenancy)
were positively related to household technical efficiency.

◇ 退耕还林政策与黄土高原地区农户可持续生计：基于生产率和效率的实证研究
Grain for Green Program and Sustainable Agriculture and Rural Livelihoods of the Loess
Plateau in China: Empirical Studies with Measurement of Productivity and Efficiency

There is a negative relationship between *Conservation_ payments* and household efficiency. Due to the significance of this parameter, we discuss it in detail. Theoretically, household technical efficiency can be affected by conservation payments which alleviate the possible liquidity constraint facing the rural households and enable their investment in more profitable farming technologies and their participation in more remunerative activities, including off – farm employment. Some empirical studies found evidence that farmers' liquidity constraints were relaxed with the introduction of GfG. Agricultural practices were moving from subsistence farming towards more intensive higher – return cash crops (Xie et al. , 2006; Uchida et al. , 2009), with improved management practices and increased capital inputs (Yao et al. , 2010), and the labor force was shifting towards off – farm employment (Uchida et al. , 2009; Groom et al. , 2010; Yao et al. , 2010; Kelly and Huo, 2013; Yin et al. , 2014; Zhen et al. , 2014). All these changes contribute to more efficient use of labor, capital and the remaining land resources and adoption of productivity – enhancing technologies, thus would increase household technical efficiency. However, the growing involvement of family members in off – farm work might compete for household labor and capital that would otherwise be allocated to agricultural land investment and technology improvements, especially in the presence of market failure which is so prevalent in developing countries (Rozelle et al. , 1999; Holden et al. , 2004; Feng, 2008; Pfeiffer et al. , 2009). And in this case, the contribution of off – farm income to household income might be compromised. Unless the contribution of off – farm income to household income outweighs the lost – labor and capital effect, off – farm employment won't contribute to increased household efficiency. Moreover, conservation payments resemble the characteristics of a decoupled subsidy (payments that are irrelevant to current production or price), which may induce a wealth effect that allows farmers to work less while maintaining consumption levels (Donnellan and Hennessy, 2012), inhibiting them from working on or off the farm. While the wealth effect has been widely tested and verified in empirical studies of decoupled subsidies (e. g., Ahearn et al., 2006; El – Osta et al., 2008; Bojnec and Latruffe, 2013), it is generally of less concern under GfG. The conspicuous exception is found the work of Liang et al. (2012), which claimed to find a negative relationship between subsidies and on – farm and off – farm income. The negative relationship of conservation payments on household efficiency indicates the possibility that conservation payments (or compensational subsidies) from the government might have a wealth effect which discourages farmers from exerting more effort into their production activities than in the absence of subsidies (Donnellan and Hennessy, 2012), or off – farm employment, as facilitated by the program, competes labor and capital in agricultural production and the effect outweigh its possible positive contribution to household income (Pfeiffera et al., 2009). According to Reardon et al. (1994) and Holden et al. (2004), the compete effect of off – farm employment on labor and capital would only happen with the existence of labor market failures, e. g., high transaction cost of searching for off – farm jobs, or failure to find a decent paid off – farm job with poor information or infrastructure.

Child – care spares total family time at home (in our study it is not possible to separate the time spent on farming with that on housework and child – care) and families with children are more likely to face off – farm employment constraints because of the high cost of living, urban schooling in towns and cities, and all these affect their optimal time allocation (Liang et al. , 2012), this might be a possible reason for the negative relationship between *Child* and household technical efficiency.

Both the *Tenancy* and *Credit* variables are positively related to household technical efficiency. Access to the market for rented farmland makes it possible to optimize farmland size or to better allocate the resources thus improving household technical efficiency. And improving farm households' access to credit may also help them apply efficient production equipment, adopt improved fertilizers or insecticides, facilitate off-farm participation, and better allocate the resources thus improving productive efficiency at the household scale (Feng, 2008; Zhao and Barry, 2014).

The results from quantile regression in the remaining columns of Table 7 - 3 reveal that the independent variables have different impacts on household efficiency across the whole distribution of the efficiency scores. For example, the negative impact of *Conservation_ payments* on household technical efficiency, is not significant at the 40th quantile but becomes significant at the right tail of distribution at the 60th and 80th quantile, one interpretation of which might be that the wealth effect does not hold for the households in the lower part of the efficiency distribution, or put it in another way, the conservation payments are not so bad to those households with poor performance or those in poverty. The quantile regression also points to a more nuanced effect of *Extension* for households in the lower part of the efficiency distribution than was revealed by the statistically insignificant OLS estimate, which might suggest that providing extension services, including technical guidance and assistance is of significance for the low-performing households. OLS suggests a negative relationship between *Child* and household technical efficiency, the quantile analysis shows that the impact is significant across all the distribution quantile and getting stronger and stronger towards the right tail of the distribution, which argues for more attention to address the issue.

7.5   Conclusions

The results of the study suggest that farm household technical efficiency and scale efficiency under VRS is averaged at 0.669 and 0.555, respectively, which suggest ample room exist to take more efficient use of the resources and technologies, and improve scale efficiency. The majority of the households show nature of increasing returns to scale, which suggests expanding their operating scales would improve their scale efficiency. Regression analysis shows that conservation payments as received by GfG participating households seems likely to induce a wealth effect, or suffer from labor market failures, which reduce their household technical efficiency, and this impact is especially significant for those households with higher performance. The presence of children in the household might also inhibits household members' efforts in farm and off – farm activities and thus decrease household efficiency, and the negative impact is also worsening with quantiles. Access of the households to market, including land lease and credit market, however, seems to benefit farm households' efficient allocation of resources, improve productivity – enhancing investments and technologies and thus improve household technical efficiency. Proving extension services also benefit those households with lower performance.

To ensure the program to achieve its intended goals to promote a sus-

◇ 退耕还林政策与黄土高原地区农户可持续生计：基于生产率和效率的实证研究
Grain for Green Program and Sustainable Agriculture and Rural Livelihoods of the Loess
Plateau in China: Empirical Studies with Measurement of Productivity and Efficiency

tainable livelihood for the farm households in the future, our study suggest better target of poor, low – performing households and proving extension services to them; removing the barriers of the farm households to land, labor and credit market, instead of throwing huge amounts of money into subsidizing them for conserving the land; either improvement in childcare arrangements in rural areas or better social security systems for migrant – worker in the cities are also suggested.

Chapter 8   Discussion, General Conclusion and Policy Implications

An extensive theoretical and empirical literature on rural households in the developing countries has argued that the existence of imperfect markets and institutions drives inefficient allocation choices, which in turn contribute to both poverty and environmental degradation (e. g., Grosjean and Kontoleon, 2009; Uchida et al., 2009; Groom et al., 2010). For example, studies in China found that liquidity constraints coupled with the failure of the off – farm labor market discourage surplus farm labor from seeking off – farm employment. Liquidity constraints also prevent farmers from investing in more profitable and capital – intensive farming technologies (Feder et al., 1990). The consequences not only include poverty, but also over – cultivation and overgrazing. These inappropriate land – use practices may have significant negative environmental externalities, such as floods and dust storms.

Severe drought in 1997 and a devastating flood in 1998, which claimed thousands of lives and caused billions of yuan of damage, finally galvanized the Chinese government into action in 1999. GfG was launched in Shaanxi, Sichuan and Gansu provinces, to prevent unsustainable agricultural prac-

◇ 退耕还林政策与黄土高原地区农户可持续生计：基于生产率和效率的实证研究

Grain for Green Program and Sustainable Agriculture and Rural Livelihoods of the Loess Plateau in China: Empirical Studies with Measurement of Productivity and Efficiency

tices. Loess Plateau, with its serious land degradation and poverty problem, is among one of the areas attached more importance. For the purpose of moving the rural areas towards sustainable development, the program's priority has been put on the maintenance or improvement of the agricultural productivity with the shrunk land area, and the transference of the surplus labor force into off – farm labor market. The main instrument of the program in the first phase was payment for ecosystem services, in which the government provides direct government subsidy (or compensation) to the participant farms in the form of cash, grain or seedling (for afforestation) for the converted land. Other side – measures were also taken in some areas in the form of proving extension visits, taking water – and – soil conservation measures (such as the land terracing in our study area), sponsoring off – farm opportunities, facilitating rural credits, etc.

Productivity and efficiency provide significant implications for more effective implementation of the program to fulfil its commitment toward sustainable agriculture and rural livelihoods of the participating farm households. Consequently, quantifying the productivity and efficiencies (changes), exploring the driving forces and identifying the determinant factors are of importance for providing sound policy advice for the follow – up implementation of the program.

The objectives of this book are to shed some light on issues related to the impact of GFG program on participating rural households' agricultural production and general household livelihoods, especially on the productivity and efficiency at the farm and farm – household level. We are concerned that: a. What changes has been induced by the program on TFP and technical efficiency of the participating farms for the agricultural production? And what factors contributed to improved TFP? b. How efficient are the farms' agricultural production under the prevailing circumstances, including the emerging technology and shrinkage of land area, etc. , brought about by the program? c. Whether the program has really promoted off – farm employment participation? What factors contributed to increased off – farm employment? Whether have the program actually contributed to improve household welfare? d. How is the performance of the households' utilizing use of its available technology and resources to maximize its household income and welfare? And what factors might contribute to improved household income and welfare?

8. 1   Main Findings, Conclusions and Policy Implications

The above – mentioned questions were answered with four case studies. To save space, the details were omitted and the following four major conclusions can be drawn from the findings of the book:

(1) Total factor productivity for the participant farms suggest great improvement after 8 years' implementation of the program, deriving from the improvement in technology. The technical efficiency against the improved technology decreased. Substantial inefficiency existed both at the farm level and farm – household level after the execution of the program.

(2) For agricultural production, soil and water conservation practices like land terracing and land consolidation, contribute significantly to agricultural TFP growth, technological improvement and technical efficiency improvement.

◇ 退耕还林政策与黄土高原地区农户可持续生计：基于生产率和效率的实证研究
Grain for Green Program and Sustainable Agriculture and Rural Livelihoods of the Loess
Plateau in China: Empirical Studies with Measurement of Productivity and Efficiency

（3）Conservation payments show no significant impact on households' off – farm participation and household welfare for off – farm non – participants, but have a significantly negative impact on household welfare for off – farm participant households. The analysis of technical efficiency at household level also suggests that conservation payments are negatively related to household technical efficiency, and this is especially significant for those households with higher performance.

（4）Off – farm participation significantly contributed to household income and per capita household income, and significantly decreased farm productivity. And it is very likely that off – farm work competes with farm work for labor and other resources.

（5）Generally speaking, access of the households to market (including land lease and credit market) and extension services, however, seems to be positively related to technical efficiency at both the farm and farm – household level.

While the results of the book are only suggestive, given the small sample size on which many of the regressions are based, they carry important policy implications nevertheless. First, better targeting of poorer households, those challenged by childcare obligations, or illiteracy is needed to fulfill GfG mandate. Second, instead of throwing huge amounts of money into subsidizing farm households for conserving the land, greater emphasis should be placed on facilitating off – farm job participation and magnifying its impact on household welfare. Third, the substitute effect between off – farm activities and farm activities indicates the possible tradeoff between livelihood diversification and food security and that greater attention to the challenge of improved farm productivity is required for the sake of food security. And finally, the implications suggest an alternative agricultural policy orientation that includes better childcare arrangements; education, training, extension services, and other human capital increasing initiatives; improved transportation infrastructure; and improving and facilitating access to land, labor, and credit markets for smallholders.

8. 2　Contributions and Limitations of the Book

The contributions of this book are largely empirical.

Firstly, it is a comprehensive study that analyzed the impact of GfG with estimators of productivity and efficiency. While previous studies have focused on the impact of the program on either farm or off – farm production, we are pondering the need to consider the farm and off – farm activities at the same time in the presence of manifold market failures. Chavas et al. (2005) proposed that the market failures present in developing countries lead to non – separability in the household technologies underlying farm and nonfarm activities justifying a household level technical efficiency analysis. But both the theoretical model studies and empirical applications of the farm – household efficiency analysis are still quite scant. By estimating technical efficiency for households participating in GfG, the analysis captures the ability of these households to obtain the maximum possible household output with a specified endowment of inputs (land, labor and capital), given existing technology and environmental conditions. It provides important information on the extent to which households have achieved sustainable livelihoods and how these sustainable livelihoods may be further improved in future.

◇ 退耕还林政策与黄土高原地区农户可持续生计：基于生产率和效率的实证研究
Grain for Green Program and Sustainable Agriculture and Rural Livelihoods of the Loess
Plateau in China: Empirical Studies with Measurement of Productivity and Efficiency

Secondly, conservation payments serve as the most important strategy in GfG program. By subsidizing farmers who agree to set aside sloping marginal land, the program is designed to induce labor and land reallocation through the liquidity effect so that sustainable livelihoods are generated and environmental services are restored. However, conservation payment, as a kind of decoupled subsidy, might also induce wealth effect which inhibits the farmers to exert more effort in farm and off - farm activities. And this has rarely been given to consideration. Comprehensive research of the impact of conservation payments is missing. The book fills in this gap. We also checked the varied impacts of conservation payments on different groups (quantiles) of households. The results show that the impact of subsidy on farm production, off - farm participation and on household welfare is either insignificant or negative. This warns us the economic impact of the program might be questionable. This has important implications because the next round of subsidy might start in few years.

Thirdly, the problem of unobserved heterogeneity has been neglected in previous studies. The difference between household welfare before and after the program, or the difference between income of participants and non - participants, might partly arise due to unobserved heterogeneity (e. g. , households participating in the program or in off - farm employment might have characteristics quite different from those of non - participants) . Neglecting the effect of unobserved heterogeneity could lead to biased estimates and misleading policy implications. When empirically examining the factors that influence household decisions to participate in off - farm work and estimate the impact of participation on household welfare, we take advantage of the ESR regression analysis method to account for unobserved heterogeneity of the off – farm participation decision that may confound its impacts on household welfare. Treatment and heterogeneity effects of off – farm participation on household welfare were also estimated explicitly within the ESR framework.

Lastly, by addressing major barriers or market failures (including land, labor and credit markets) that impede farmers' efficient allocation choices other than by compensating households for conserving sloping land, the book sheds new light on the most effective policy options to achieve the program's goals.

We should admit, however, the research in this book suffers from serious flaw of limited sample size and data inconsistency, which should be addressed in future studies.

Reference

[1] Abay, C. , et al. An Analysis of Input Use Efficiency in Tobacco Production with Respect to Sustainability: The Case Study of Turkey [J]. Journal of Sustainable Agriculture, 2004, 24 (3): 123 – 143.

[2] Ahearn, M. C. , et al. The Impact of Coupled and Decoupled Government Subsidies on Off Farm Labour Participation of U. S. Farm Operators [J] . American Journal of Agricultural Economics, 2006, 88 (2): 393 – 408.

[3] Alem, Y. , et al. Improving Welfare Through Climate – Friendly Agriculture: The Case of the System of Rice Intensification [J]. Environmental and Resource Economics, 2015, 62 (2): 243 – 263.

[4] Alene, A. D. , Zeller, M. Technology Adoption and Farmer Efficiency in Multiple Crops Production in Eastern Ethiopia: A Comparison of Parametric and Non – Parametric Distance Functions [J] . Agricultural Economic Review, 2005, 6 (1): 5 – 17.

[5] Altieri, M. A. Agroecology: A New Research and Development – Paradigm for World Agriculture [J] . Agriculture, Ecosystems & Environment, 1989, 27 (1 – 4): 37 – 46.

[6] Alvarez, A. , Arias, C. Technical Efficiency and Farm Size: A Conditional Analysis [J]. Agricultural Economics, 2004, 30 (3):

241 – 250.

[7] Amaza, P. S. , Ogundari, K. An Investigation of Factors That Influence the Technical Efficiency of Soybean Production in the Guinea Savannas of Nigeria [J]. Journal of Food, Agriculture and Environment, 2008, 6 (1): 92 – 96.

[8] Appleton, S. , Balihuta, A. Education and Agricultural Productivity: Evidence from Uganda [J]. Journal of International Development, 1996, 18 (3): 172 – 175.

[9] Ash, R. F. , Edmonds, R. L. China's Land Resources, Environment and Agricultural Production [J] . The China Quarterly, 1998 (156): 836 – 879.

[10] Ashley, C. , Maxwell, S. Rethinking Rural Development [J]. Development Policy Review, 2001, 19 (4): 395 – 425.

[11] Banker, R. D. , et al. Some Models for Estimating Technical and Scale Inefficiencies in Data Envelopment Analysis [J]. Management Science, 1984, 30 (9): 1078 – 1092.

[12] Banker, R. D. , Natarajan, R. Evaluating Contextual Variables Affecting Productivity [J] . Operations Research, 2008, 56 (1): 48 – 58.

[13] Barbier, E. B. The Concept of Sustainable Economic Development [J] . Environmental Conservation, 1987, 14 (2): 101 – 110.

[14] Barbier, E. B. , et al. Sustainable Agricultural Development and Project Appraisal [J]. European Review of Agricultural Economics, 1990, 17 (2): 181 – 196.

[15] Bauer, B. W. , et al. Consistency Conditions for Regulatory Analysis of Financial Institutions: A Comparison of Frontier Efficiency Methods [J] . Journal of Economics and Business, 1998, 50 (2): 85 –

◆ 退耕还林政策与黄土高原地区农户可持续生计：基于生产率和效率的实证研究
Grain for Green Program and Sustainable Agriculture and Rural Livelihoods of the Loess
Plateau in China: Empirical Studies with Measurement of Productivity and Efficiency

114.

［16］Becker, B. Sustainability Assessment: A Review of Values, Concepts, and Methodological Approaches ［R］. Issues in Agriculture. CGIAR, World Bank, 1997.

［17］Benjamin, D. , Brandt, L. Property Rights, Labour Markets, and Efficiency in a Transition Economy: The Case of Rural China ［J］. Canadian Journal of Economics, 2002, 35 (4): 689 – 716.

［18］Beyene, A. D. Determinants of Off – farm Participation Decision of Farm Households in Ethiopia ［J］. Agrekon, 2008, 47 (1): 140 – 161.

［19］Binam, J. N. , et al. Factors Affecting the Technical Efficiency among Smallholder Farmers in the Slash and Burn Agriculture Zone of Cameroon ［J］. Food Policy, 2004, 29 (5): 531 – 545.

［20］Birkhaeuser, D. , et al. The Economic Impact of Agricultural Extension: A Review ［J］. Economic Development and Cultural Change, 1991, 39 (3): 607 – 650.

［21］Bishop, R. C. Economic Efficiency, Sustainability, and Biodiversity ［J］. Ambio, 1993, 22 (2): 69 – 73.

［22］Bojnec, S˘. , Latruffe, L. Farm Size, Agricultural Subsidies and Farm Performance in Slovenia ［J］. Land Use Policy, 2013 (32): 207 – 217.

［23］Bravo – Ureta, B. E. , Pinheiro, A. E. Efficiency Analysis of Developing Country Agriculture: A Review of the Frontier Function Literature ［J］. Agricultural and Resource Economic Review, 1993, 22 (1): 88 – 101.

［24］Burton, S. Land Consolidation in Cyprus: A Vital Policy for Rural Construction ［J］. Land Use Policy, 1988, 5 (1): 131 – 147.

[25] Callens, I. , Tyteca, D. Towards Indicators of Sustainable Development for Firms: A Productive Efficiency Perspective [J]. Ecological Economics, 1999, 28 (1): 41 –53.

[26] Cao, S. X. , et al. Impact of China's Grain for Green Project on the Landscape of Vulnerable Arid and Semi – Arid Agricultural Regions: A Case Study in Northern Shaanxi Province [J]. Journal of Applied Ecology, 2009, 46 (3): 536 –543.

[27] Caves, D. W. , et al. The Economic Theory of Index Numbers and the Measurement of Input, Output, and Productivity [J]. Econometrica, 1982, 50 (6): 1393 –1414.

[28] CGIAR. Sustainable Agricultural Production: Implications for International Agricultural Research [R]. Report of the Technical Advisory Committee, CGIAR. Washington D. C. , 1988.

[29] Charles, A. F. Sustainable Agriculture: Myths and Realities [J]. Journal of Sustainable Agriculture, 1990, 1 (1): 97.

[30] Chavas, J. P. , et al. Farm Household Production Efficiency: Evidence from the Gambia [J]. American Journal of Agricultural Economics, 2005, 87 (1): 160 –179.

[31] Chen, L. , et al. Land – Use Change in a Small Catchment of Northern Loess Plateau, China [J]. Agriculture, Ecosystems & Environment, 2001, 86 (2): 163 –172.

[32] Chen, Z. , et al. Farm Technology and Technical Efficiency: Evidence from Four Regions in China [J]. China Economic Review, 2009, 20 (2): 153 –161.

[33] Cheng, L. , Liu, J. Influences of Grain for Green Project on Food Security in China [J]. Journal of Beijing Forestry University (Social

◇ 退耕还林政策与黄土高原地区农户可持续生计：基于生产率和效率的实证研究
Grain for Green Program and Sustainable Agriculture and Rural Livelihoods of the Loess
Plateau in China: Empirical Studies with Measurement of Productivity and Efficiency

Science), 2007, 6 (4): 42 - 47.

[34] Cheng, L., et al. The Effects of Grain for Green Project on the County - level Food Security in the Loess Plateau Hilly Region—A Case Study in Mizhi, Qingjian, Zizhou and Wupu Counties of Shaanxi Province [J]. Journal of Natural Resources, 2010, 25 (10): 1689 - 1697 (In Chinese).

[35] Clark, W. C., Dickson, N. M. Sustainability Science: The Emerging Research Program [J]. Proceedings of the National Academy of Sciences, 2003, 100 (14): 8059 - 8061.

[36] Coelli, T. A Guide to DEAP Version 2. 1: A Data Envelopment Analysis Computer Program [R]. Working Paper 96/08. Center for Efficiency and Productivity Analysis, University of New England, Australia, 1996.

[37] Coelli, T. J., et al. An Introduction to Efficiency and Productivity Analysis [M]. New York: Springer, 2005.

[38] Conway, G. Agroecosystem Analysis [M]. London: Imperial College, 1983.

[39] Conway, G. The Properties of Agroecosystems [J]. Agricultural Systems, 1987, 24 (2): 95 - 117.

[40] Conway, G. The Doubly Green Revolution: Food for All in the Twenty - First Century [M]. New York: Comstock Publishing Associates, 1997.

[41] Dai, Q., et al. Health Diagnoses of Ecosystems Subject to a Typical Erosion Environment in Zhifanggou Watershed, North - West China [J]. Frontiers of Forestry in China, 2007, 2 (3): 241 - 250.

[42] Dang, X., et al. Ecological Economic Coupling Process and Sustainability for Ecological Rehabilitation of Xiannangou Catchment in the Loess

Hilly Region [J]. Acta Ecologica Sinica, 2008, 28 (12): 6321 –6333.

[43] Davis, B. , et al. Rural Nonfarm Employment and Farming: Household – Level Linkages [J]. Agricultural Economics, 2009, 40 (2): 119 – 123.

[44] Debreu, G. The Coefficient of Resource Utilization [J]. Econometrica, 1951 (19): 273 –292.

[45] Deininger, K. , Jin, S. Land Rental Markets as an Alternative to Government Reallocation? Equity and Efficiency Considerations in the Chinese Land Tenure System [J]. China Economic Quarterly, 2004, 119 (2): 678 –704.

[46] De Janvry, A. , Sadoulet, E. Progress in the Modeling of Rural Households' Behavior under Market Failures [M]. New York: Springer, 2006.

[47] Delang, C. O. , Yuan, Z. China's Grain for Green Program: A Review of the Largest Ecological Restoration and Rural Development Program in the World [M]. Heidelberg: Springer, 2015.

[48] Deng, X. Z. , et al. Cultivated Land Conversion and Potential Agricultural Productivity in China [J] . Land Use Policy, 2006, 23 (4): 372 –384.

[49] Donnellan, T. , Hennessy, T. Defining a Theoretical Model of Farm Households' Labour Allocation Decisions [R] . Centre for European Policy Studies, 2012.

[50] Duraiappah, A. K. Poverty and Environmental Degradation: A Review and Analysis of the Nexus [J]. World Development, 1998, 26 (12): 2169 –2179.

[51] Ehui, S. K. , Spencer, D. S. C. Measuring the Sustainability

❖ 退耕还林政策与黄土高原地区农户可持续生计：基于生产率和效率的实证研究
Grain for Green Program and Sustainable Agriculture and Rural Livelihoods of the Loess
Plateau in China： Empirical Studies with Measurement of Productivity and Efficiency

and Economic Viability of Tropical Farming Systems： A Model from Sub -
Saharan Africa ［J］. Agricultural Economics，1993，9（4）：279 -296.

［52］ El - Osta，H. ，et al. Off - farm Labor Participation Decisions of
Married Farm Couples and the Role of Government Payments ［J］. Review
of Agricultural Economics，2008，30（2）：311 -332.

［53］ Enders，C. ，Bandalos，D. The Relative Performance of Full Information Maximum Likelihood Estimation for Missing Data in Structural Equation Models ［J］. Structural Equation Modeling，2001，8（3）：430 -457.

［54］ Fan，S. ，Zhang，X. Infrastructure and Regional Economic Development in Rural China ［J］. China Economic Review，2004，15（2）：
203 -214.

［55］ Fan，S. ，et al. Returns to Public Agricultural and Rural Investments in China ［J］. China Agricultural Economic Review，2018，10
（2）：215 -223.

［56］ FAO. The Den Bosch Declaration and Agenda for Action on Sus-
tainable Agriculture and Rural Development： Report of the Conference ［R］.
FAO Conference on Agriculture and the Environment's Hertogenbosch，
Netherlands，1991.

［57］ Färe，R. ，et al. Productivity Developments in Swedish Hospi-
tals： A Malmquist Output Index Approach ［A］// Charnes，A. ，et al.
（Eds. ）Data Envelopment Analysis： Theory，Methodology and Applications ［C］. Boston： Kluwer Academic Publishers，1994a.

［58］ Färe，R. ，et al. Productivity Growth，Technical Progress，and
Efficiency Change in Industrialized Countries ［J］. American Economic Re-
view，1994b，84（5）：66 -83.

［59］ Färe，R. ，et al. Production Frontiers ［M］. Cambridge： Cambridge University Press, 1994c.

[60] Farrell, M. The Measurement of Productive Efficiency [J]. Journal of the Royal Statistical Society, 1957, 120 (3): 253 – 290.

[61] Feder, G. , et al. The Relationship Between Credit and Productivity in Chinese Agriculture: A Microeconomic Model of Disequilibrium [J]. American Journal of Agricultural Economics, 1990, 72 (4): 1151 – 1157.

[62] Feng, Z. M. , et al. Grain – for – Green Policy and Its Impacts on Grain Supply in West China [J]. Land Use Policy, 2005, 22 (4): 301 – 312.

[63] Feng, S. Land Rental, Off – farm Employment and Technical Efficiency of Farm Households in Jiangxi Province, China [J]. Wageningen Journal of Life Sciences, 2008, 55 (4): 363 – 378.

[64] Fernandez – Cornejo, J. Off – farm Income, Technology Adoption, and Farm Economic Performance [R]. Economic Research Report 30, USDA, 2007.

[65] Fletschner, D. Women's Access to Credit: Does It Matter for Household Efficiency? [J]. American Journal of Agricultural Economics, 2008, 90 (3): 669 – 683.

[66] Fried, H. , et al. Efficiency and Productivity [A] // Fried, H. , et al. (Eds.) . The Measurement of Productive Efficiency and Productivity Change [C]. New York: Oxford University Press, 2008.

[67] Groom, B. , et al. Relaxing Rural Constraints: A "Win – Win" Policy for Poverty and Environment in China? [J]. Oxford Economic Papers, 2010, 62 (1): 132 – 156.

[68] Grosjean, P. , Kontoleon, A. How Sustainable Are Sustainable

◇ 退耕还林政策与黄土高原地区农户可持续生计：基于生产率和效率的实证研究

Grain for Green Program and Sustainable Agriculture and Rural Livelihoods of the Loess Plateau in China: Empirical Studies with Measurement of Productivity and Efficiency

Development Programs? The Case of the Sloping Land Conversion Program in China [J]. World Development, 2009, 37 (1): 268 – 285.

[69] Guo, L., et al. Species Diversity and Interspecific Association in Development Sequence of Hippophae Rhamnoides Plantations in the Loess Hilly Region, China [J]. Frontiers of Biology in China, 2008, 3 (4): 489 – 495.

[70] Heckman, J., et al. Four Parameters of Interest in the Evaluation of Social Programs [J]. Southern Economic Journal, 2001, 68 (2): 210 – 223.

[71] Hennessy, T. C., Rehman, T. Assessing the Impact of the "Decoupling" Reform of the Common Agricultural Policy on Irish Farmers' Off – farm Labour Market Participation Decisions [J]. Journal of Agricultural Economics, 2008, 59 (1): 41 – 56.

[72] Hoff, A. Second Stage DEA: Comparison of Approaches for Modeling the DEA Score [J]. European Journal of Operational Research, 2007, 181 (1): 425 – 435.

[73] Holden, S. T., et al. Non – farm Income, Household Welfare, and Sustainable Land Management in a Less – Favoured Area in the Ethiopian Highlands [J]. Food Policy, 2004, 29 (4): 369 – 392.

[74] Huang, J., et al. Moving off the Farm and Intensifying Agricultural Production in Shandong: A Case Study of Rural Labor Market Linkages in China [J]. Agricultural Economics, 2010, 40 (2): 203 – 218.

[75] Huang, Z., Zhang, X. Preliminary Analysis of Productivity and Realization Approaches of Main Grain Crops on the Loess Plateau [J]. North – West Soil Erosion Research Quarterly, 1989, 10 (1): 168 (In Chinese).

[76] Huffman, W. E. , Lange, M. D. Off – farm Work Decisions of Husbands and Wives: Joint Decision Making [J]. Review of Economics and Statistics, 1989, 71 (3): 471 –480.

[77] Jiao, J. , et al. Factors Affecting Distribution of Vegetation Types on Abandoned Cropland in the Hilly – Gullied Loess Plateau Region of China [J]. Pedosphere, 2008, 18 (1): 24 –33.

[78] Jorgenson, D. W. , Griliches, Z. The Explanation of Productivity Change [J] . Review of Economic Studies, 1967, 34 (3): 249 –283.

[79] Karagiannis, G. , Sarris, A. Measuring and Explaining Scale Efficiency with the Parametric Approach: The Case of Greek Tobacco Growers [J] . Agricultural Economics, 2005, 33 (Supp.): 441 –451.

[80] Kelly, P. , Huo X. Land Retirement and Nonfarm Labor Market Participation: An Analysis of China's Sloping Land Conversion Program [J]. World Development, 2013 (48): 156 –169.

[81] Koenker, R. , Bassett, G. Regression Quantiles [J]. Econometrica, 1978, 46 (1): 33 –50.

[82] Komarek, A. M. , et al. Household – Level Effects of China's Sloping Land Conversion Program under Price and Policy Shifts [J]. Land Use Policy, 2014 (40): 36 –44.

[83] Komatsu, Y. , et al. Evaluation of Agricultural Sustainability Based on Human Carrying Capacity in Drylands—A Case Study in Rural Villages in Inner Mongolia, China [J]. Agriculture, Ecosystems & Environment, 2005, 108 (1): 29 –43.

[84] Koopmans, T. Activity Analysis of Production and Allocation [M]. New York: John Wiley and Sons Inc. , 1951.

[85] Kuntashula, E. , Mungatana, E. Estimating the Causal Effect

◆ 退耕还林政策与黄土高原地区农户可持续生计：基于生产率和效率的实证研究
Grain for Green Program and Sustainable Agriculture and Rural Livelihoods of the Loess
Plateau in China：Empirical Studies with Measurement of Productivity and Efficiency

of Improved Fallows on Farmer Welfare Using Robust Identification Strategies in Chongwe, Zambia ［J］. Agroforestry Systems, 2013, 87 （6）：1229 – 1246.

［86］ Latruffe, L. , et al. Application of a Double Bootstrap to Investigation of Determinants of Technical Efficiency of Farms in Central Europe ［J］. Journal of Productivity Analysis, 2008, 29 （2）：183 – 191.

［87］ Leibenstein, H. Allocative Efficiency VS. "X – Efficiency" ［J］. American Economic Review, 1966 （56）：392 – 415.

［88］ Lewandowski, I. M. , et al. Sustainable Crop Production：Definition and Methodological Approach for Assessing and Implementing Sustainability ［J］. Crop Science, 1999, 39 （1）：184 – 193.

［89］ Li, L. , et al. Efficiency and Its Determinant Factors for Smallholder Farms in the Grain for Green Program on the Loess Plateau, China ［J］. Journal of Food, Agriculture and Environment, 2010, 17 （4）：20 – 24.

［90］ Li, L. , et al. Conservation Payments, Off – farm Employment and Household Welfare for Farmers Participating in "Grain for Green" Program in China ［J］. China Agricultural Economic Review, 2019, 12 （1）：71 – 89.

［91］ Liang, Y. , et al. Does Household Composition Matter? The Impact of the Grain for Green Program on Rural Livelihoods in China ［J］. Ecological Economics, 2012, 75 （2）：152 – 160.

［92］ Lin, G. C. S. , Ho, S. P. S. China's Land Resources and Land – Use Change：Insights from the 1996 Land Survey ［J］. Land Use Policy, 2003, 20 （2）：87 – 107.

［93］ Liu, G. Soil Conservation and Sustainable Agriculture on the Loess Plateau: Challenges and Prospective [J]. Ambio, 1999, 28 (8): 663 – 668.

[94] Liu, Q. , et al. Poverty Reduction within the Framework of SDGS and Post – 2015 Development Agenda [J]. Advances in Climate Change Research, 2015, 6 (1): 67 – 73.

[95] Liu, Y. Pushed out or Pulled In? Participation in Non – farm Activities in Rural China [J]. China Agricultural Economic Review, 2017, 9 (1): 111 – 129.

[96] Lokshin, M. , Sajaia, Z. Maximum Likelihood Estimation of Endogenous Switching Regression Models [J]. The Stata Journal, 2004, 4 (3): 282 – 289.

[97] Lopez, S. , et al. Sustainable Evaluation: Applying Ecological Principles and Tools to Natural Resource Management Systems [A]// Prado – Lorenzo, J. (Ed.) Sustainable Development: New Research [C] . New York: Nova Science Publishers, 2006.

[98] Lovo, S. Income Diversification, Access to Liquidity and Farm Household Technical Efficiency—Evidence from South Africa [R]. The 5th PHD Presentation Meeting of the Royal Economic Society. 16 – 17th January, the Department of Economics, City University, London, 2010.

[99] Lynam, J. K. , Herdt, R. W. Sense and Sustainability: Sustainability as an Objective in International Agricultural Research [J]. Agricultural Economics, 1989, 3 (4): 381 – 398.

[100] Maddala, G. S. Limited – Dependent and Qualitative Variables in Econometrics [M]. Cambridge: Cambridge University Press, 1983.

[101] Malmquist, S. , Index Numbers and Indifference Surfaces [J]. Trabajos De Estatistica, 1953, 4 (2): 209 – 242.

◆ 退耕还林政策与黄土高原地区农户可持续生计：基于生产率和效率的实证研究
Grain for Green Program and Sustainable Agriculture and Rural Livelihoods of the Loess
Plateau in China： Empirical Studies with Measurement of Productivity and Efficiency

［102］ Martinez – Cordero, F. J. , Leung, P. S. Sustainable Aquaculture and Producer Performance： Measurement of Environmentally Adjusted Productivity and Efficiency of a Sample of Shrimp Farms in Mexico ［J］. Aquaculture, 2004, 241 （1 – 4）： 249 – 268.

［103］ Masters, W. A. , Shively, G. E. Economic Efficiency in Farm Households： Trends, Explanatory Factors, and Estimation Methods ［J］. Agricultural Economics, 2010, 40 （5）： 587 – 599.

［104］ Matshe, I. , Young, T. Off – farm Labour Allocation Decisions in Small – scale Rural Households in Zimbabwe ［J］. Agricultural Economics, 2004, 30 （3）： 175 – 186.

［105］ Mcdonald, J. Using Least Squares and Tobit in Second Stage DEA Efficiency Analyses ［J］. European Journal of Operational Research, 2009, 197 （2）： 792 – 798.

［106］ Mueller, S. Evaluating the Sustainability of Agriculture： The Case of the Reventado River Watershed in Costa Rica ［R］. European University Studies, Series 5, Economics and Management Peter Lang, Germany, 1997.

［107］ Murgai, R. , et al. Productivity Growth and Sustainability in Post – Green Revolution Agriculture： The Case of the Indian and Pakistan Punjabs ［J］ . World Bank Research Observations, 2001, 16 （2）： 199 – 218.

［108］ National Bureau of Statistics of China. Statistical Data ［DB/OL］. Http： //www. stats. gov. cn/tjsj/, 2008.

［109］ Nehring, R. , Fernandez – Cornejo, J. The Impacts of Off – farm Income on Farm Efficiency, Scale, and Profitability for Corn Farms ［C］ . Annual Meeting, American Agricultural Economics Association,

Providence, Ri 19566, 2005.

[110] Oseni, G. , Winters, P. Rural Nonfarm Activities and Agricultural Crop Production in Nigeria [J]. Agricultural Economics, 2009, 40 (2): 189 – 201.

[111] Owusu, V. , et al. Non – farm Work and Food Security Among Farm Households in Northern Ghana [J]. Food Policy, 2011, 36 (2): 108 – 118.

[112] Paul, C. J. M. , Nehring, R. Product Diversification, Production Systems, and Economic Performance in U. S. Agricultural Production [J]. Journal of Economics, 2005, 126 (2): 525 – 548.

[113] Pearce, D. , et al. Sustainable Development Economics and Environment in the Third World [M]. London: Earthscan, 2000.

[114] Peng, H. , et al. Social, Economic, and Ecological Impacts of the Grain for Green Project in China: A Preliminary Case in Zhangye, Northwest China [J]. Journal of Environmental Management, 2007, 85 (3): 774 – 784.

[115] Pfeiffer, L. , et al. Is Off – farm Income Reforming the Farm? Evidence from Mexico [J]. Agricultural Economics, 2009, 40 (2): 125 – 138.

[116] Plucknett, D. , Smith, N. Sustaining Agricultural Yields [J]. Bioscience, 1986, 36 (1): 40 – 45.

[117] Pugh, C. Sustainability, the Environment, and Urbanization [M]. London: Earthscan, 1996.

[118] Rahman, S. , Rahman, M. Impact of Land Fragmentation and Resource Ownership on Productivity and Efficiency: The Case of Rice Producers in Bangladesh [J]. Land Use Policy, 2008, 26 (1): 95 – 103.

◇ 退耕还林政策与黄土高原地区农户可持续生计：基于生产率和效率的实证研究
Grain for Green Program and Sustainable Agriculture and Rural Livelihoods of the Loess
Plateau in China: Empirical Studies with Measurement of Productivity and Efficiency

［119］ Reardon, T. , et al. Links Between Nonfarm Income and Farm Investment in African Households: Adding the Capital Market Perspective ［J］.
American Journal of Agricultural Economics, 1994, 76 (5): 1172 –1176.

［120］ Reardon, T. African Agriculture: Productivity and Sustainability Issues ［A］// Eicher, C. K. , Staatz, J. M. (Eds.) . International Agricultural Developmen (3rd Ed.)［C］. Baltimore: The Johns Hopkins University Press, 1998.

［121］ Rozelle, S. , et al. Migration, Remittances, and Agricultural
Productivity in China ［J］. American Economic Review, 1999, 89 (2):
287 –291.

［122］ Ruttan, V. Constraints on the Design of Sustainable Systems of
Agricultural Production ［J］. Ecological Economics, 1994, 10 (3): 209 –
219.

［123］ Scoones, I. Sustainable Rural Livelihoods: A Framework for
Analysis ［R］. IDS Working Paper No. 72, Brighton: IDS, 1998.

［124］ Shi, H. , Shao, M. Soil and Water Loss from the Loess Plateau
in China ［J］. Journal of Arid Environments, 2000, 45 (1): 9 –20.

［125］ Shi, X. Heterogeneous Effects of Rural – Urban Migration on
Agricultural Productivity ［J］. China Agricultural Economic Review, 2018,
10 (3): 482 –497.

［126］ Simar, L. , Wilson, P. W. A General Methodology for Bootstrapping in Nonparametric Frontier Models ［J］. Journal of Applied Statistics, 2000, 27 (6): 779 –802.

［127］ Singh, I. , et al. Agricultural Household Models: Extensions,
Applications, and Policy ［M］. Baltimore: The Johns Hopkins University
Press, 1986.

[128] Solís, D. , et al. Technical Efficiency among Peasant Farmers Participating in Natural Resource Management Programmes in Central American [J] . Journal of Agricultural Economics, 2009, 60 (1): 202 –219.

[129] State Council of the P. R. C. Circular of the Ministry of Water Resources on Strengthening Recent Opinions on Flood Control Construction of Yangtze River [EB/OL]. National Release, 1999, No. 12.

[130] State Council of the P. R. C. Sloping Land Conversion Program Regulations [EB/OL] . National Release, 2002, No. 367. Http: // www. forestry. gov. cn/main/434/20101101/448755. html.

[131] State Council of the P. R. C. Notice on Combing with Other Five Initiatives and Further Consolidating the Achievements of the Conversion of Farmland to Forestland Program [EB/OL]. National Release, 2005, No. 25. Http: //www. gov. cn/zhengce/content/2008 –03/28/content_ 2799. htm.

[132] State Council of the P. R. C. Notice on the Improvement of the Policy and Measures of the Conversion of Farmland to Forestland Program [EB/OL]. National Release, 2007, No. 25. Http: //www. gov. cn/zhengce/ content/2008 –03/28/content_ 2767. htm.

[133] State Council of the P. R. C. Sloping Land Conversion Program Regulations (Revised Version) [EB/OL]. National Release, 2016, No. 666. Http: //www. gov. cn/zhengce/2020 –12/26/content_ 5573517. htm.

[134] SFA, MOLAR, SMF. Announcement on the Pilot Projects of the Grain for Green Program on the Middle and Upper Reaches of the Yellow River Basin and Upper Reaches of the Yangtze River Basin [EB/OL]. 2000, No. 111. Http: //www. forestry. gov. cn/main/434/20101101/448773. html.

[135] SFA, NFGA. Announcement on the Measures for the Manage-

◆ 退耕还林政策与黄土高原地区农户可持续生计：基于生产率和效率的实证研究
Grain for Green Program and Sustainable Agriculture and Rural Livelihoods of the Loess
Plateau in China： Empirical Studies with Measurement of Productivity and Efficiency

ment of Funds for Forestry Ecological Protection and Restoration ［EB/OL］.
2018， No. 66. Http：//www. gov. cn/xinwen/2018 – 07/26/content＿ 5309391.
htm.

［136］ Solow， R. Contribution to the Theory of Economic Growth ［J］.
Quarterly Journal of Economics， 1956， 70 （1）： 65 – 94.

［137］ Solow， R. Technical Change and the Aggregate Production Function ［J］ . Review of Economics and Statistics， 1957， 39 （3）： 312 – 320.

［138］ Taddese， G. Land Degradation： A Challenge to Ethiopia ［J］.
Environmental Management， 2001， 27 （6）： 815 – 824.

［139］ Tan， S. ， et al. Impact of Land Fragmentation on Rice Producers' Technical Efficiency in South – East China ［J］. Wageningen Journal
of Life Sciences， 2010， 57 （2）： 117 – 123.

［140］ Tauer， L. W. ， Nazibrola， L. Farmer Efficiency and Technology
Use with Age ［J］. Agricultural and Resource Economic Review， 2000， 29
（1）： 24 – 31.

［141］ Tiongco， M. ， Dawe， D. Long – Term Evolution of Productivity
in a Sample of Philippine Rice Farms： Implications for Sustainability and
Future Research ［J］. World Development， 2002， 30 （5）： 891 – 898.

［142］ Tisdell， C. Sustainable Development： Differing Perspectives of
Ecologists and Economists， and Relevance to LDCS ［J］. World Develop-
ment， 1988， 16 （3）： 373 – 384.

［143］ Tsunekawa， A. ， et al. Restoration and Development of the
Degraded Loess Plateau， China ［M］. Tokyo： Springer， 2014.

［144］ Uchida， E. ， et al. Grain for Green： Assessing the Cost – effectiveness and Sustainability of China's Conservation Set – aside Program
［J］ . Land Economics， 2005， 81 （2）： 247 – 264.

[145] Uchida, E. , et al. Are the Poor Benefiting from China's Land Conservation Program? [J]. Environment and Development Economics, 2007, 12 (4): 593 –620.

[146] Uchida, E. , et al. Conservation Payments, Liquidity Constraints and Off – farm Labor: Impact of the Grain for Green Program on Rural Households in China [J]. American Journal of Agricultural Econo-mics, 2009, 91 (1): 70 –86.

[147] United Nations. Report of the United Nations Secretary – General, Implementation of the Third United Nations Decade for the Eradication of Poverty (2018 –2027) [R]. Https: //undocs. org/a/75/280, 2018.

[148] UNCED. Report of the United Nations Conference on Environment and Development [R]. Document A/Conf. 151/26/Rev. 1 – Vol. 1 – Un Publication Sales No. E. 93. I. 8, 1992.

[149] Wang, C. , et al. Evaluation of the Economic and Environmental Impact of Converting Cropland to Forest: A Case Study in Dunhua County, China [J]. Journal of Environmental Management, 2007, 85 (3): 746 –756.

[150] WECD. Our Common Future (The Bruntland Report): World Commission on Environment and Development [M]. New York: Oxford University Press, 1987.

[151] Weitzman, M. L. Sustainability and Technical Progress [J]. Scandinavian Journal of Economics, 1997, 99 (1): 1 –13.

[152] Welch, F. Education in Production [J]. Journal of Political E-conomics, 1970, 78 (1): 35 –59.

[153] Wooldridge, J. Econometric Analysis of Cross Section and Panel Data (2nd Ed.) [M]. Cambridge MA: MIT Press, 2010.

◆ 退耕还林政策与黄土高原地区农户可持续生计：基于生产率和效率的实证研究
Grain for Green Program and Sustainable Agriculture and Rural Livelihoods of the Loess
Plateau in China: Empirical Studies with Measurement of Productivity and Efficiency

[154] Wu, B. , et al. Yellow River Basin Management and Current Issues [J]. Journal of Geographical Science, 2004, 14 (1): 29 –37.

[155] Wunder, S. , et al. Taking Stock: A Comparative Analysis of Payments for Environmental Services Programs in Developed and Developing Countries [J]. Ecological Economics, 2008, 65 (4): 834 –852.

[156] Xie, C. , et al. Livelihood Impacts of the Conversion of Cropland to Forest and Grassland Program [J]. Journal of Environmental Planning and Management, 2006, 49 (4): 555 –570.

[157] Xu, Z. , et al. China's Sloping Land Conversion Program Four Years on: Current Situation, Pending Issues [J]. International Forestry Review, 2004, 6 (3): 317 –326.

[158] Xu, J. , et al. China's Ecological Rehabilitation: Unprecedented Efforts, Dramatic Impacts and Requisite Policies [J]. Ecological Economics, 2006, 57 (4): 595 –607.

[159] Xu, J. , et al. China's Sloping Land Conversion Program: Does Expansion Equal Success? [J]. Land Economics, 2010, 86 (2): 219 –244.

[160] Xu, Z. , et al. Grain for Green Versus Grain: Conflict Between Food Security and Conservation Set – aside in China [J]. World Development, 2006, 34 (1): 130 –148.

[161] Yao, S. , et al. An Empirical Analysis of the Effects of China's Land Conversion Program on Farmers' Income Growth and Labor Transfer [J]. Environmental Management, 2010, 45 (3): 502 –512.

[162] Yin, R. , et al. The Implementation and Impacts of China's Largest Payment for Ecosystem Services Program as Revealed by Longitudinal Household Data [J]. Land Use Policy, 2014 (40): 45 –55.

[163] Zhang, S. , et al. Impacts of Compensation Policies in Refo-re-station Programs [R] . Report of the Environment and Poverty Programme to China Council for International Cooperation in Environment and Develop-ment, 2005.

[164] Zhao, J. , Barry, P. J. Effects of Credit Constraints on Rural Household Technical Efficiency [J]. China Agricultural Economic Review, 2014, 6 (4): 654 –668.

[165] Zhen, N. , et al. Changes of Livelihood Due to Land Use Shifts: A Case Study of Yanchang County in the Loess Plateau of China [J]. Land Use Policy, 2014 (40): 28 –35.

[166] Zhou, S. , et al. The Costs and Benefits of Reforestation in Li-ping County, Guizhou Province, China [J] . Journal of Environmental Management, 2007, 85 (3): 722 –735.